Praise for THE VOLA

MW01487667

"As Americans have less and less discretionary money it is now even more difficult to build for a successful retirement. This strategy allows for more aggressive investing, quality lifetime retirement income and legacy planning, all the while protecting for long-term care. All with the same dollars! Every American should read this book!"

VAN MUELLER, LUTCF

"David McKnight's new book depicts many Americans' misconceptions about average rates of return and sustainable withdrawal rates in retirement. It also illustrates the critical importance of the timing of one's returns during the distribution phase of retirement. Having a properly funded volatility shield is critical to the success of anyone's retirement plan. This story is a must read!"

JOHN W. WHEELER, JR. CFP®, CLU, CHFC, CRPC®, LUTCF, WATER TOWER FINANCIAL PARTNERS, LLC, CHICAGO, IL

"Once again, David McKnight delivers! In The Volatility Shield *he explains the dangerous impact of market volatility on retirement income. Through the experience of Jack Wheeler we learn how to bypass the limitations of traditional withdrawal rates without running out of money. A must read for any investor saving for retirement."*

–PAUL MURRAY, AIF, CHFC, CDFA, WEALTH & ADVISORY ASSOCIATES, LLC, CHALFONT, PA

"David McKnight has the unique ability of taking a complex financial concept and making it simple and easy to understand. Because this book reads like a novel, you enjoy the story and learn valuable financial insights along the way."

–LANE MARTINSEN, RFC, RICP, MARTINSEN WEALTH MANAGEMENT, LLC, CHANDLER, AZ

"I was familiar with the volatility shield concept before I read this book, but David explains it in an intriguing, story-based format. The plot was engaging while at the same time driving home important financial principles. This is a must read whether you have just begun to save for retirement or are an experienced investor!"

–JENNIFER BAKER, CPA, RICP, BAKER WEALTH STRATEGIES, CYPRESS, TX

"David has written a thought-provoking story that should strike a nerve. This refreshingly quick read speaks volumes about the financial headwinds facing so many as they plan for retirement. His simple solution provides the security everyone should aspire to in their retirement years. Follow Jack Wheeler on his journey of financial awareness."

—CARROLL RAMER, RAMER RETIREMENT SOLUTIONS, ROCHESTER, MN

"This wonderful story pulled me in and always had me guessing what was going to happen next. Its compelling narrative teaches important financial principles while its heartfelt conclusion will bring a tear to your eye. This is a must read for my clients."

—BILL ROE, PIONEER WEALTH MANAGEMENT, ASHEVILLE, NC

"In The Volatility Shield, *common misconceptions regarding average rates of return and the 4% Rule are dealt with in a way every person can understand. Seventy-five percent of retirees and pre-retirees are afraid of either not having enough money or running out of money before they die. This book tells you how to solve those problems."*

—THOMAS O'CONNELL, INTERNATIONAL FINANCIAL ADVISORY GROUP, INC., ROCKAWAY, NJ

*"*The Volatility Shield *is beautiful. I read it in one sitting and never thought of putting it down. The story brought home the powerful impact a volatility shield can have on your retirement. The math is presented so clearly anyone can understand it."*

—CLYDE CLEVELAND, IWG INVESTMENT ADVISORS, LLC, FORT LAUDERDALE, FL

*"*The Volatility Shield *should be required reading for anyone interested in comprehensive retirement planning. Too often we focus solely on the accumulation phase, thinking the same rules apply during the distribution phase of retirement. The truth is, when you begin taking withdrawals in retirement, the rules of the game change.* The Volatility Shield *uses a compelling story to help illustrate this very important point."*

—MICHELLE GESSNER, CFP, GESSNER WEALTH STRATEGIES, LLC, HOUSTON, TX

"David McKnight's wonderful novella communicates vital truths about how to ensure financial security in retirement. His writing style will open your mind to options you have not likely heard from most advisors in the financial services industry. A compelling read."

—Lauren Gidley, Prosperity Wealth Management, Williamsville, NY

The Volatility Shield is a very timely and true to life picture of what many Americans will go through in retirement. An excellent read and well worth the short time it takes to get the whole picture. Excellent novella, David!"

—James Bertine, Knights of Columbus, Springfield, VA

"David McKnight's story of how Jack Wheeler comes to understand the implications of withdrawal rates and sequence of return risk is indispensable to all those looking to maximize their retirement income. The way McKnight explains the concept of the 'volatility shield' is innovative and irrefutable!"

—Randy Cowell, CFP, ACT Financial Services, Tulsa, OK

The Volatility Shield will open your eyes to the toll sequence of returns can take on your retirement portfolio. David McKnight outlines the perfect solution to weathering negative stock market returns during retirement. Loved it!"

—Arthur Athanas, Impact Wealth Group, LLC, Fort Lauderdale, FL

"David McKnight does a fantastic job of drawing you in, while at the same time explaining a strategy that most investors have never encountered. This book will not only change your life in retirement, but the lives of your children as well."

—Paul Seal, Ascendant Wealth Strategies, Burke, VA

"In a fun and engaging story David has outlined a strategy vital to retirement planning. He has demonstrated how, with proper planning, retirees can better navigate the volatility of markets and safely increase their potential retirement income streams."

—Walter C Young III, MBA, Pacific Capital Resource Group, Inc., Seattle, WA

Also by David McKnight:

THE POWER OF ZERO
LOOK BEFORE YOU LIRP

A FINANCIAL NOVELLA

THE VOLATILITY SHIELD

How to Vanquish the 4% Rule &
Maximize Your Retirement Income

David McKnight

This book is dedicated to my family.
They are my rock and my lodestar.

CONTENTS

CHAPTER 1

Jack Wheeler punched the accelerator on his 1996 Chevy Impala as he tore past city limits. With his hometown squarely in his rear-view mirror, a giddiness began to wash over him. His Masters of Engineering degree was firmly in hand, and he was about to step into his first post-college job over 3,000 miles away in San Jose, California. He could finally close the chapter on Lancaster, North Carolina, and its most famous resident.

Within seconds, he was humming along the freeway, flirting with nine over the limit. When he reached for the radio, he saw his cell-phone vibrate to life on the console below. Someone had left a message. Strange. He hadn't heard the phone ring. He put in his Bluetooth earpiece, then dialed his voicemail. When he heard the voice, his spirits cratered.

"Hey, Jack, it's your stepdad, Ted. I hope I'm not too late, but I'd really like to see you before you head west. It's urgent. Swing by the office as soon as you can."

Jack cursed under his breath. Ted Hardy had been the driving force behind his decision to move to the west coast in the first place.

As much as he loved being near his mom, the sooner he could put distance between himself and Ted, the better. His mom would always be welcome to visit. Alone.

He drove another five miles, doing his best to ignore Ted's message, but when he came to the next exit, he found his car veering towards it. Within 15 minutes, he was pulling into the parking lot at Hardy's Sporting Goods.

Jack weaved his way through the aisles of hockey sticks and tennis rackets until he made it to Ted's sprawling executive suite in the back corner of the store. On the wall behind Ted's desk were framed newspaper articles, along with faded pictures of Ted from the early '80s throwing passes and eluding defenders. There was even a plaque from when Ted had garnered NFC Offensive Player of the Week honors. Jack had always thought of this office as Ted's shrine to himself, a constant reminder to all who entered that Ted Hardy was once an elite NFL quarterback. Jack wasn't going to miss this office one bit.

Ted sat reclined in his chair, his face buried in the latest edition of ESPN magazine. When Jack entered, Ted looked up and flashed a perfunctory smile. "Jack, my boy, take a seat."

Jack bristled as he slid into the chair opposite Ted and folded his arms tightly against his chest.

"You said it was urgent," Jack said. "I was on my way out of town when you called, so I'm already losing time. Can we make this quick?"

Ted flashed another smile. It was that same look he wore in his TV spots when he was selling something no one really needed. Jack had learned to be supremely distrustful of that smile.

"Look, Jack," Ted said, the smile cracking slightly. "I just wanted to let you know that I'm sorry about how things have gone down. I haven't been the easiest guy to live with these past ten years. Just wanted to say that you're welcome back any time."

Ted extended his hand for a conciliatory handshake.

"You could've said that over the phone," Jack said, eyeing the hand warily.

"I like to look a man in the eye when I make amends."

Jack hesitated another moment, then took Ted's hand in his own and gave it a few weak pumps.

"Good luck with everything," Ted said.

"Thanks," Jack said, managing a weak smile. He let go and began to rise from his chair.

"Say, before you leave, I was wondering if you might give me a hand with something."

Jack collapsed back into his chair, barely stifling a laugh. There it was: *the catch*. With Ted, there was always some ulterior motive lurking right around the corner.

"I know you're on a tight schedule, but I could really use your help before you hit the road."

"What do you want?" Jack breathed.

"It's about the business," Ted said. "Sold it off last week. All seven stores. The sale price was almost $4 million, and I'll net about $3 million after tax."

"Congratulations," Jack said coolly.

"I got retirement projections from Bruce Lassiter today," Ted continued. "He says the projections are conservative and practically guarantee I'll never run out of money. I'm not so sure. I'm only 50, so I need this money to last 35, maybe 40, years. I don't want to adopt a plan if it's not sustainable. You mind taking a peek?"

Jack had always been good with numbers and had even minored in finance, but he was reluctant to give Ted financial planning advice on the fly.

"I don't know, Ted, I really need to be going."

"Come on, Jack. It'll take five minutes. It's not just my future on the line here but Genny's, too."

With the mention of his mother Jack collapsed back into his chair. "All right, I'll take a look," he said with a sigh.

Ted slid the proposal across the table. Jack picked it up and scrutinized the rows of numbers. After a few minutes, he looked back at Ted.

"Looks like he's recommending you take $165,000 out every year for the next 35 years. He's also running this projection at an annual average rate of return of 9%. Do you think that's realistic?"

"Bruce claims his average annual rates of return since 1990 have been over 14%. Seems like I should be able to do 9% standing on my head."

Jack shrugged. Nine percent seemed doable given the trend in the stock market over the last decade, but he also knew it could all turn on a dime.

"Nine percent might be pushing it a skosh, but in the big scheme of things, you'll probably be okay. And if the most you ever take out is $165,000 per year, you'll never eat into your $3 million principal. At least, not in theory."

"Bruce calls it the 'set it and forget it' plan. Set this thing in motion, take your distributions, then ride off into the sunset. And that's what I want for Genny and me: a worry-free retirement. Do *you* think that's what these numbers will achieve?"

Jack looked over the proposal again. "I think it's a sound plan. Average rates of return *are* a tad aggressive. But, if you *can* average 9% per year, *and* you and Mom keep your pre-tax lifestyle at or below $165,000 every year, then you should never run out of money."

Ted slapped his hand down on the table with satisfaction. "That's what I needed to hear! I appreciate you stopping by, Jack."

Ted rose and gave Jack's hand another shake.

"Thanks again, Jack. I owe you one."

Jack pressed his lips into a thin, hard line before he bid Ted goodbye and strode toward the door. When his hand touched the doorknob, he paused for a moment and then wheeled around. Their relationship would never be any better than it was right now. He had nothing to lose.

"Can I cash in that favor *now*?"

Ted had already settled back into his magazine. "Shoot," he said, without bothering to look up.

"When I was in college, I worked over at the Lancaster Boys Club. We took kids from rough neighborhoods, single-parent homes, and gave them mentors, a safe environment, and a standing invitation to play pickup basketball. I spent a few years there myself before you and Mom got married. Mel Kauffman founded it nearly a decade back. Do you remember him?"

"Mel Kauffman. I can't seem to shake that guy. He's like one of those little yippers who grabs on to the cuff of your pants and won't let go. Stops by every month or so asking for money. Finally got to the point where I had to ask him not to come by at all."

Jack's determination to keep peace with his stepfather was quickly fading. "Right. Well, these kids are transforming under his leadership. He's changing all of their lives for the better."

"Okay," Ted said. He raised his eyes from his magazine and fixed them warily upon Jack. "What about it?"

"Their facility needs some major overhauls: re-varnish the basketball court, replace the backboards, fix the air conditioning. You get the idea. Would you ever be open to emceeing a fundraising event? Sign some memorabilia, pose for pictures?"

Ted grimaced. "Yeah, I don't know, Jack."

"Ted, if they don't get an infusion of cash soon, they may have to close their doors. That won't be good for those boys, and it certainly won't be good for the town of Lancaster."

Ted let out a long, exasperated stream of pent-up air.

"I love a noble cause just like the next guy," Ted said. "But if I say yes to Mel Kauffman, the floodgates open. I do that one for free, then who's next? Before I know it, I'm spending all my waking moments handing out freebies. And that's just not how I want to spend the next chapter of my life. Remember, Jack: *worry-free* retirement."

"But it's a worthwhile…" Jack trailed off. Ted had already buried his nose back in his magazine. "Never mind."

He turned around and stormed out of Ted's office. Once again, Ted had given Jack a poignant reminder of why he was leaving Lancaster and never coming back.

CHAPTER 2

Nineteen Years Later

"Okay, kids, 30 seconds and we load into the car," came the warning call from Jack's wife, Chloe. Jack began wrangling his three kids toward the door when the buzz of a cellphone stopped him in his tracks. He looked back at it warily. After a brief pause, he worked his way back to the kitchen counter, grabbed his phone and then pushed it up to his face.

It was his stepsister.

"It's Annie," he told Chloe, giving her a knowing glance.

"You better take it in the study," Chloe said over her shoulder as she corralled their children onto the front porch.

Jack loved his stepsister, but whenever Annie called, it was never about catching up. Since their mom Genevieve had died of ovarian cancer ten years earlier, her calls had always had a central theme: it was time to make peace with Ted. She'd insisted that Ted had changed, that Genny's death had softened him. But whenever Jack asked if Ted had begun to leverage his celebrity for charity, the answer was always no. In other words, Ted hadn't really changed at all.

"Hi, Annie," Jack said, with all the feigned cheer he could muster.

"Jack, you have to come home." The hard edge in her voice made it sound like a command.

"Annie, we've been over this. I don't—"

"It's Ted. He…"

Jack's heart dropped into his stomach.

"What happened?" he asked, his gut tightening.

"He's in critical condition. You have to come. Quickly."

Jack paused for a beat before responding. "Annie, I'm really sorry, but—"

"You're his financial power of attorney," Annie hissed. "Important decisions have to be made. I know you hated my dad, but you have an obligation to fulfill."

To everyone's surprise, Ted had named Jack as both financial power of attorney and executor of his estate shortly after his mother's death. Jack had scoffed at the email when he'd received it, then he'd quickly forgotten about it. Annie obviously hadn't.

Jack took a deep, labored breath. "I'll take the first flight out."

* * *

Even at 69, Ted Hardy had been full of vigor. He'd always looked after himself and, according to the latest reports from Annie, was in top physical form. The figure that lay before Jack, surrounded by a chaos of wires and whirring machines, was a husk of a man. Only the blip of the monitor and the subtle rise and fall of Ted's chest betrayed any signs of life.

Behind Jack, a door swung open. He wheeled around to see a man in a white lab coat stride in, manila folder in hand. It was Dr. Abbott Sidwell, Ted's long-time physician. He put a comforting hand on Jack's shoulder and gave it a soft squeeze, but his face was grim.

"Thank you for flying out so quickly," the doctor said in hushed tones.

"What's his status?" Jack asked, his voice quavering. Seeing Ted's inert figure had provoked a maelstrom of emotions that left him surprisingly shaken.

Dr. Sidwell pulled him to the side. His eyes conveyed the seriousness of what he was about to say. Jack's stomach pooled into concrete.

"There's no easy way to say this. Your stepfather had an aneurism while watching his grandson's football game. We did everything we could, but he's lost a lot of brain function. His condition isn't immediately life-threatening, but from a cognitive perspective, he'll never be the same. His condition…it's irreversible."

"He won't *ever* recover?"

"I'm afraid not. And while Ted will live, he'll be lucky to make it two years, three tops."

Jack shook his head as a surreal feeling washed over him.

"I know this is all happening very quickly," Dr. Sidwell continued, "but you should secure his long-term living arrangements while you're in town. I understand you're the financial power of attorney?"

"That's right."

"Good. Your stepfather will need full-time care. He'll eventually regain consciousness, but he won't be able to communicate or act for himself. All the more important that you find a facility where he'll be comfortable and receive good care."

"Some sort of long-term care facility?"

"That's right."

Jack felt a heavy numbness invade his limbs. "What are his choices?"

"In town, there are two options when it comes to long-term care facilities. Sunset Senior Care over on Walnut is the best. He'll get fine care there. It isn't cheap, but they have an impeccable reputation."

"And the second option?" Jack asked.

"Well, it *is* an option, but not an attractive one. St. Luke's over on Fifth. It's a Medicaid-funded facility. Paid for by the state. Bare-bones type care. For the indigent, it's their only option. But for someone like Ted Hardy, Sunset is the obvious choice. The only choice, really. Costs will run about $10,000 per month. That will be partially offset by his Social Security, but Ted's estate will have to handle the rest."

Jack nodded. If there was one thing Ted was not short of, it was money. With the growth of the stock market over the last 19 years, and his trademark tightfistedness, there would almost certainly be enough money for Ted to live out his few remaining years with the best care money could buy.

* * *

Jack stepped out of the hospital lobby and bent into the chilly November wind. As he strode across the parking lot, a shadow approached in his periphery. Jack turned and saw a heavyset man in his mid-fifties with thick glasses and a nest of dark, curly hair. He was brandishing a recording device.

"Sal Giordano from the Gazette," the man said as he approached. "How is he?"

"How is who?" Jack asked without slackening his pace.

"Ted Hardy. Witnesses saw him collapse at a youth football game." Sal was trying to match Jack's stride, but he was already falling behind.

"This is a private family matter," Jack said over his shoulder. "I'll thank you to give us some space."

Jack arrived at his car but struggled to fish his keys out of his pocket. It gave Sal just enough time to catch up.

"All-American quarterback at Nebraska. Starting quarterback for the Chicago Bears and later the Los Angeles Rams. 'The Legend of Lancaster.' I think this community deserves to be apprised of his condition."

"It's a private family matter," Jack repeated, this time more forcefully.

Sal tsked-tsked through coffee-stained teeth. "I have sources all over this town. It's just a question of time before the truth comes out. This is your chance to shape the narrative from the start."

"No comment," Jack said as he folded himself into the front seat of his rental car and grabbed for the door. Sal had already wedged himself against it.

"If Ted survives this health crisis, whatever it is, there's a good chance he'll end up in one of two places: either Sunset or St. Luke's. Where he ends up depends entirely upon the state of his finances. How *are* his finances, by the way?"

All at once, Jack understood Sal's angle. There was nothing more titillating than a sports legend who had retired with millions only to spend his waning years in a Medicaid-funded long-term care facility. His home town of Lancaster would be scandalized.

"Ted's far from broke, if that's what you're insinuating."

Sal flashed a disingenuous smile. "Well, let's certainly hope so. We idolize our heroes, and it's always so heart-wrenching when they fail to live up to it. Brings a tear to the eye just thinking about it."

CHAPTER 3

As Jack drove to Ted's condo, deep anger fanned out across his chest. There was no love lost between him and Ted, but Sal was clearly the type of journalist who would do anything for a salacious story. Jack white-knuckled the steering wheel as he tamped down his anger. He needed to train his sights on his most pressing task: assessing Ted's financial picture, and then arranging for payment at Sunset Senior Care.

As he drove, he began roughing out Ted's likely expenses at Sunset Senior Care in his head. His Social Security was probably in the area of $2,000 per month, net of taxes. He'd have to liquidate an additional $8,000 per month, net after tax over the course of his stay. Given a three-year stint, it would end up costing Ted almost $400,000. This would drain what little savings most Americans had in a matter of months. But not Ted. Jack thought back to those projections he had reviewed 19 years earlier. If they'd held up, and Jack was sure that they had, Ted's net worth would hardly feel the strain.

* * *

Jack stepped into Ted's condo and took in his surroundings. The walls were white and bare save for a few cheap paintings hung limply askew. The furniture was sparse and second-hand. It was a glaring contrast from the home that Ted and Genevieve had lived in prior to her death. Something about it seemed off.

He made his way back to his stepfather's office and collapsed into a vinyl chair in front of an enormous oak desk. The desk had been the lone holdover from Ted's days at the sporting goods store. It was a massive desk. Larger than life. A bit like Ted's personality, Jack mused.

He looked at the computer screen on the desk and noticed a post-it note with a single word written on it: genevieve. His mom. He felt a well of emotion spring up within him. The pain of watching her slow fade into oblivion had been indelibly etched into his heart. The cancer had been brutal and had ravaged her body for nearly six months before carrying her away.

As much as Jack chafed at Ted's massive ego and selfishness, there was no denying how Ted had felt about his mother. After reminiscing for a moment, Jack returned to the matter at hand. Within weeks, Sunset would be expecting the first month's payment, and he had to determine which assets to liquidate. Jack's first phone call would go to Bruce Lassiter's office.

Jack pulled the heavy oak file drawer open and quickly located an expandable file labeled "Finances." Within it, he found a hanging folder labeled "Retirement." It was brimming with unopened envelopes, each of which bore the logo for Lassiter Financial. Jackpot.

He pulled out the envelope at the front of the folder, opened it, and retrieved the statement inside. As he scanned for a phone number, his eyes slid down the page and alighted on a set of bolded letters and numbers at the bottom of the statement: **TOTAL PORTFOLIO VALUE: $71,198.**

Puzzled, Jack flipped the page over, scanning for more numbers, other accounts. Surely, this wasn't all Ted had left. These figures were supposed to be bigger. Much bigger. Jack rifled frantically through all the other pages, but there were *no* other numbers.

That was it…$71,198.

Jack's memory once again carried him back to the projections Ted had shown him in his office at Hardy's Sporting Goods. Jack had scrutinized Bruce's projection and concluded that so long as Ted took out $165,000 per year, and averaged 9% per year or better, he'd never run out of money. That left only two possibilities. Either Ted had gone on a bender and had burned through his fortune, or Bruce Lassiter had done much worse than 9%.

Jack's nerves simmered at a low buzz as he picked up his phone and charged toward the door. Given the stakes, he had no choice but to confront Bruce Lassiter in person.

*   *   *

"Can I help you?" a middle-aged woman asked from behind an expensive granite counter. Her name plate identified her as Janice.

"Hi, Janice. I need to see Bruce Lassiter. It's urgent."

"I apologize, but Mr. Lassiter is on an important phone call right now, and then he's booked back to back for the rest of the afternoon. Perhaps I can leave a message for him?"

"My stepfather, Ted Hardy, has had a major health crisis, and I'm in town to shore up his financial situation." He took the financial power of attorney paperwork out of his bag and pushed it across the counter. "I need to talk to Bruce as quickly as possible."

Janice was obviously caught off guard by the news. "I'm so sorry to hear about Ted. I hope he'll be all right. He's done so much for this practice over the years. Maybe I can just poke my head into Mr. Lassiter's office."

She disappeared around the corner, and, within two minutes, she was back.

"Mr. Lassiter said that he's aware of Ted's health situation. He had a grandson who was there when Ted collapsed. He passes along his most sincere condolences."

Janice's smile was thin and strained. Jack could sense something was amiss.

"You don't seem to understand," Jack said. "I'm in town for a very short time, and I need to see Bruce before I go. Go back there and tell him that I won't leave until he sees me."

"I'm afraid Mr. Lassiter is booked for the rest of the week. Maybe there's something *I* can help you with?" Janice said, hoping to prevent an escalation.

Jack stood there, hands flat on the counter, his frustration mounting. There was no way he was waiting until the following Monday to confront Bruce about the pitifully low balance in Ted's account.

"All right," Jack said, "if you *do* want to help, this is what I'm going to need. I need to see Ted's rates of return, year by year, for the last 19 years. Then I need to see documentation of all of his distributions over that same time frame."

The tension drained from Janice's face. "That *is* something I can do for you. Why don't you take a seat and I'll have those ready in just a few minutes."

Jack collapsed into one of the chairs behind him, his mood darkening by the moment. He suspected that Bruce's "packed schedule" was more about his unwillingness to face the music about Ted's average rates of return. He was clearly adept at avoiding angry clients demanding answers about their underperforming portfolios. Within five minutes, Janice reappeared with an orange envelope in her hand. She handed it to Jack.

"On the first sheet, you'll find the year by year returns going back to the year 2000 along with the average annual rate of return in bold at the bottom of the page. The other sheets show all of Ted's distributions going back to the beginning."

Jack thanked her, wheeled around, and charged out of the office.

CHAPTER 4

Back at Ted's condo, Jack tore the envelope open and let its contents spill onto the desk before him. First, he grabbed the rate of return sheet. His eyes fell to the bottom of the page where he saw the average annual rate of return in bold type: **8.1%**. He pulled out his calculator, added up all the returns over the last 19 years, then divided by 19. Sure enough, 8.1%. This was almost a full point lower than what had been projected on the retirement plan he'd examined 19 years earlier. Could that have been enough to bankrupt Ted's portfolio? Jack didn't know yet. A lot of it depended on Ted's distributions since retiring at 50.

Jack began sifting through the documentation of Ted's withdrawal history. True to the original projections, Ted had made systematic withdrawals of $165,000 every year for the last 19 years. There were no deviations. The money had been withdrawn every year, even in the ten years following Genevieve's death.

Jack puzzled over these new bits of data, trying to make sense of them. If Ted's distributions never deviated from plan, then the low average rates of return had to be the reason for the massive hole in Ted's portfolio.

He fired up his laptop and opened up a blank Excel spreadsheet. Within a few minutes, he'd created a calculator with five columns: one for the year, one for the beginning of the year account balance, one for average annual rate of return, one for annual pre-tax distributions, and one for the end of the year account balance.

When he was done he hit enter, and then held his breath as the numbers flashed across his screen.

Year	Beginning of Year Account Value	Earnings Rate	Annual Cash Cash Flow	End of Year Account Value
2000	$3,000,000	8.10%	-$165,000	$3,064,635
2001	$3,064,635	8.10%	-$165,000	$3,134,505
2002	$3,134,505	8.10%	-$165,000	$3,210,035
2003	$3,210,035	8.10%	-$165,000	$3,291,683
2004	$3,291,683	8.10%	-$165,000	$3,379,945
2005	$3,379,945	8.10%	-$165,000	$3,475,355
2006	$3,475,355	8.10%	-$165,000	$3,578,494
2007	$3,578,494	8.10%	-$165,000	$3,689,987
2008	$3,689,987	8.10%	-$165,000	$3,810,511
2009	$3,810,511	8.10%	-$165,000	$3,940,797
2010	$3,940,797	8.10%	-$165,000	$4,081,637
2011	$4,081,637	8.10%	-$165,000	$4,233,884
2012	$4,233,884	8.10%	-$165,000	$4,398,464
2013	$4,398,464	8.10%	-$165,000	$4,576,375
2014	$4,576,375	8.10%	-$165,000	$4,768,696
2015	$4,768,696	8.10%	-$165,000	$4,976,595
2016	$4,976,595	8.10%	-$165,000	$5,201,334
2017	$5,201,334	8.10%	-$165,000	$5,444,278
2018	$5,444,278	8.10%	-$165,000	$5,706,899

Jack's eyes drew wide. He checked his numbers and equations to make sure the figures were correct. Then he checked them again. The numbers never changed. The $165,000 annual distributions with an average annual return of 8.1% would have put Ted's balance at over $5.7 million by the end of 2018. Almost double where he started! That was a far cry from $71,000!

Jack's hands drew into fists. There was over $5.6 million in Ted's portfolio that couldn't be accounted for, 5.6 million reasons for Bruce Lassiter to avoid meeting with Jack face to face. Jack couldn't shake the feeling that so long as he was in town, Bruce's schedule would remain conveniently full of appointments.

But before leveling any hasty accusations, Jack wanted to look for any other clues that might explain why Ted's once robust portfolio had dwindled to a paltry $71,000. He turned to the financial file and began flipping through it again. The first label that caught his eye was life insurance. He browsed through the file and produced a 30-year term insurance policy for $500,000. According to the policy, it had been taken out when Ted was 41 with a premium of $36 per month. Was it still in force?

He tossed it onto the desk in front of him and scoured the file for more clues. Within seconds, he produced another unopened envelope. This one was from the life insurance company. He opened it up. It was a lapse notice dating back to a few months after his mother's death. Strange. Why would Ted have let his life insurance policy lapse when there were still 12 years left before it expired? The $36-a-month premium was a pittance for that kind of death benefit. Why not just ride it out?

Jack continued to search the files for any additional information but found nothing. What Jack really needed was a second set of eyes. Perhaps a more trustworthy financial advisor could help him uncover an angle that he hadn't yet considered. He wanted to have all his ducks in a row when he confronted Bruce Lassiter.

His eyes fell reflexively to the term policy lying on the desk in front of him. He picked it up and began to flip through its pages when a business card slipped out and fell onto the desk.

JANE FLETCHER
LIFE INSURANCE AGENT

The card was old and weathered. Jack doubted Jane Fletcher was even in business at this point. A life insurance salesperson from 30 years ago? The odds were clearly against it. Just for kicks, he punched her name into Google and waited for the results to appear.

After a few moments, Jane Fletcher popped onto his screen. Surprisingly, she *was* still in business. She stood in front of a colonial-style office building, surrounded by a staff of eight. Behind them, looming large, was a sign that said **Fletcher Financial**. Jane Fletcher appeared to be about 60 years old now, and, by the looks of things, her business was thriving. The website advertised money management, financial planning, retirement strategies, and, yes, life insurance.

As he studied the picture a plan began to form in his mind. Jane *had* met with Ted, even if their encounter had been nearly 30 years ago. Her success in the industry meant that she could provide additional insight into the missing money in Ted's portfolio.

Jack dialed the number on the screen.

"Fletcher Financial, this is Heather. How can I help you?"

"Hi, Heather, I'd like to make an appointment with Jane."

"Are you a client?"

"Not currently, but I am looking for a second opinion. My name is Jack Wheeler."

Heather went quiet for a moment and then said, "You're in luck, Mr. Wheeler. Jane had a cancelation for tomorrow at 10 a.m. How does that sound?"

"Perfect. I'll see you then."

Jack ended the call. It didn't look like he'd be going home anytime soon.

CHAPTER 5

Hello, Jane," Jack said, shaking Jane's hand. "I appreciate you seeing me on such short notice."

"I'm glad we found an opening for you, Mr. Wheeler. It's not usually this easy on such short notice." She was smartly dressed in a blazer and slacks and sat behind a large rectangular glass table. On the shelves behind her were pictures of children and grandchildren flashing cherubic smiles for the camera.

"Would you mind telling me a bit about your practice before we begin?" Jack asked. From what he'd seen on her website, she was perfectly qualified to provide a second opinion, but a few pointed questions would confirm it.

"Gladly," Jane said with a smile. "We've been helping people with their retirement for over 30 years. Primarily money management, some estate planning, long-term care planning, and life insurance. I graduated from UNC Chapel Hill in 1979."

Jack remembered the life insurance reference from the website. It had made him a bit uneasy. He had to ask the question before they went any further.

"You mentioned life insurance. What are we talking about here, term insurance?"

"When it's the right fit, but not always. We offer our clients permanent life insurance as well. But again, it has to be the right fit."

Jack grimaced at that. He had an unbridled contempt for permanent life insurance. It was often sold as an investment, but it was laden with onerous fees. As an engineer, and someone who was good with numbers, the math had to vindicate the strategy. And, according to the articles he'd read about permanent life insurance, the math was problematic. So, for most of his adult life, he'd been an unflinching advocate of the least expensive of all life insurance: term insurance.

"Is there something wrong?" Jane asked, her mouth curving into a frown.

"Sorry, I've just never been a big fan of permanent life insurance."

"I see." She paused for a few moments before continuing. "How is it I can help you, Mr. Wheeler?"

Given Jane's willingness to sell these types of policies, Jack questioned how useful she could be. But he was already in her office, and whatever opinion she gave could always be tossed aside if it proved to be without merit.

"A second opinion," Jack reminded her.

"Ah, yes. Heather mentioned as much. Tell me about your situation."

"My stepfather had a stroke about 48 hours ago and will need long-term care over the next two to three years. As his financial power of attorney, I'm in charge of making sure his long-term care expenses get paid. There's only one small problem: he appears to have only $71,000 to his name."

Jane gave him a troubled look. "He'll qualify for a Medicaid-funded long-term care facility within the year. Assuming he lives here in Lancaster, that would be St. Luke's over on Fifth. Is that the second opinion you were looking for?"

Jack shook his head. "I want to know why my stepfather is only worth $71,000. You see, Jane, 19 years ago he had $3 million in his account."

Jane frowned. "So, your stepfather was a big spender?"

"Quite the opposite, actually. And *that's* why I'm here. His money manager claims that he grew my stepfather's assets at an average annual rate of return of 8.1%, net of fees, over the last 19 years."

He took the sheet of returns out of his briefcase and pushed it across the desk. Her eyes scanned quickly down the page.

"The numbers just don't add up," Jack continued. "The current advisor refuses to meet with me, so I wanted to know what you thought about the situation. Maybe there's something here that I'm just not homing in on."

"Well, those annual rates of return aren't too far out of line," Jane confirmed. "Our clients' returns have been very similar over the same time frame. Not exactly the same, but in the same ballpark. So, nothing unusual there."

Jack shook his head in confusion as he reached for his laptop to show her the spreadsheet he'd created earlier.

"If you'll look at the calculator I created, you'll see why I'm so alarmed. When I plug in his starting balance, the average annual rate of return, and his annual $165,000 distribution, you'll see that he should still have well over $5 million in his account, not $71,000. What am I missing here?"

Jack had played a role, however small, in sending Ted down this path. If the plan was doomed from the start, then there might well be a massive hole in Jack's own retirement plan.

She studied him for a moment and then asked, "Does your spreadsheet allow you to input the rates of return year by year?"

Jack frowned at her unexpected reply. "Of course. It's a little more time intensive, but it's just a question of plunking them in one by one. But I don't understand the point. If he really averaged 8.1% over the last 19 years, then what you're suggesting is just busy work. It wouldn't change the outcome."

"Humor me," she said with a wink. "I'll even punch them in for you."

Jack's eyes narrowed. What she was asking for didn't seem to strike at the heart of the problem.

"Have at it, but I really don't see the point. I've checked and rechecked the math. When you add up all the rates of return and divide by the number of years, you get 8.1%."

"I understand your position, Mr. Wheeler, and you wouldn't be the first person to espouse it. But if you want to find out what happened to your stepfather's money, this is a critical first step." She said it with the calm, confident tone of someone who had gone more than a few rounds with skeptical clients over the years.

Jack muttered under his breath as he slid his laptop across the table. When she was done, she pushed the laptop back over to Jack's side of the desk.

Year	Beginning of Year Account Value	Earnings Rate	Annual Cash Cash Flow	End of Year Account Value
2000	$3,000,000	-9.17%	-$165,000	$2,575,031
2001	$2,575,031	-11.72%	-$165,000	$2,127,575
2002	$2,127,575	-24.02%	-$165,000	$1,491,164
2003	$1,491,164	28.82%	-$165,000	$1,708,365
2004	$1,708,365	11.73%	-$165,000	$1,724,402
2005	$1,724,402	5.23%	-$165,000	$1,640,958
2006	$1,640,958	15.62%	-$165,000	$1,706,503
2007	$1,706,503	4.87%	-$165,000	$1,616,574
2008	$1,616,574	-39.05%	-$165,000	$884,735
2009	$884,735	26.52%	-$165,000	$910,608
2010	$910,608	15.12%	-$165,000	$858,344
2011	$858,344	2.03%	-$165,000	$707,419
2012	$707,419	17.11%	-$165,000	$635,227
2013	$635,227	35.33%	-$165,000	$636,358
2014	$636,358	19.13%	-$165,000	$561,529
2015	$561,529	15.84%	-$165,000	$459,339

Year	Beginning of Year Account Value	Earnings Rate	Annual Cash Cash Flow	End of Year Account Value
2016	$459,339	19.21%	-$165,000	$350,882
2017	$350,882	31.41%	-$165,000	$244,267
2018	$244,267	-10.18%	-$165,000	$71,198

"How…" Jack began. "How is this possible?!" He pulled the laptop closer, focusing on the cell that Jane had highlighted. It was Ted's end of year account value in 2018. His heart plunged into his stomach like an elevator with a snapped cable.

"$71,000!" he exclaimed. "That can't be right. It *can't* be!"

"I can assure you that the numbers on that spreadsheet are exactly right, Mr. Wheeler."

"I don't know what you've done to force this result," he said stubbornly, "but this does *not* reflect an 8.1% average rate of return."

"It most certainly does."

Jack scrutinized each cell in the spreadsheet, checking and re-checking the formulas. He then highlighted all the rates of return so that the spreadsheet could calculate the average rate of return. Sure enough: 8.1%. But, how could this be?

He pushed the laptop away in disgust.

"What's wrong, Mr. Wheeler?"

"Nineteen years ago, my stepfather asked for my opinion on a financial plan that his financial advisor had given him. It called for $165,000 annual distributions and an average annual return of 9%. So long as those two variables held true, according to the plan, he would never run out of money. Well, he didn't get 9%, he only got 8.1%. But, according to *my* math, he should still be swimming in money. I'm a civil engineer, Jane. If my numbers don't add up, bridges collapse. Tell me where I went wrong."

Jane favored him with a maternal smile.

"Well, for starters, the spreadsheet you created assumed an *average* annual rate of return of 8.1%." She slid the rate of return sheet across the table to Jack. "Did your stepfather ever actually earn 8.1% in any one year?"

Jack scanned the column. "No. No, he didn't."

"That's because *average* rates of return almost never correspond to *actual* rates of return. The first mistake that you and your stepfather made was to think that average rates of return were a meaningful metric in retirement planning. That may be a useful number to someone who's trying to persuade you to hire them as your money manager. But in the real world, it serves no real purpose."

Jack grunted his displeasure as he folded his arms across his chest.

"If you want to figure out what happened to your stepfather's money, you can't focus on the *average* rate of return. You have to focus on the order in which those returns were received."

"Okay," he said cautiously. "I'm listening."

"For example, what were the rates of return in the first three years of your stepfather's retirement?"

Jack ran down the sheet. "The year 2000, -9.17%; the year 2001, -11.72%; the year 2002, -24.02%."

"And how much was he taking from his portfolio in each of those years?"

"$165,000."

"And, according to your revised spreadsheet, what was his actual balance at the end of that third year?"

Jack's gut tightened into a fist when he looked at the corresponding cell.

Year	Beginning of Year Account Value	Earnings Rate	Annual Cash Cash Flow	End of Year Account Value
2000	$3,000,000	-9.17%	-$165,000	$2,575,031
2001	$2,575,031	-11.72%	-$165,000	$2,127,575
2002	$2,127,575	-24.02%	-$165,000	$1,491,164

He swallowed hard. "A little less than $1.5 million."

"Here's the point: when you withdraw money from your portfolio in a down year, you kill the dollars that are supposed to be earning you money. In other words, you diminish the portfolio's ability to produce that income on a sustainable basis."

A tongue of acid began to lap at the back of Jack's throat. He'd come here looking for answers that would implicate Bruce Lassiter. He wasn't expecting an indictment of his own financial paradigm.

"You're telling me that the average annual rates of return that money managers brandish like a Good Housekeeping Seal of Approval are completely useless?"

"Yes, especially in retirement. You see, once you go into the distribution phase of your life, the rules of the game change. It's all about the actual rates of return and the order in which those returns are received. This is the single greatest risk a retiree can face. We call it sequence of return risk."

"Sequence of return risk?" Jack had never heard of it.

"That's right. Your stepfather hasn't been swindled, and he isn't a victim of bad money management. A money manager who, *unfortunately*, put too much attention on average rates of return? Perhaps. But not bad money management."

"Something is amiss here," Jack insisted. "I just can't quite put my finger on *what*."

"You're right Mr. Wheeler. Something *is* amiss. Your stepfather's withdrawal rates were *far* too high."

"How are you supposed to determine a safe withdrawal rate if average annual rates of return are meaningless?"

"*That* is the right question, Mr. Wheeler." There was approval in her eyes. "How *do* you determine a safe withdrawal rate in retirement?"

He stared at her blankly, and, when she didn't proffer an answer, he asked, "Well?"

"Our industry has spent years trying to figure this out. They've performed thousands of simulations that include such variables as withdrawal rates, stock allocation percentages, length of retirement, and order of returns. We call these Monte Carlo simulations."

Jack *had* heard of those.

"And after years of research," Jane continued, "they've come to a consensus on what constitutes a safe withdrawal rate in retirement."

"And that is?" Jack asked, leaning forward with genuine interest.

Jane pulled a sheet out of a drawer and pushed it across the table.

All Observations		Annualized Withdrawal Rate of as % of Initial Portfolio Value, then adjusted for CPI								
Final Asset Value Target = 0		3.00%	3.25%	3.50%	3.75%	4.00%	4.25%	4.50%	4.75%	5.00%
100% Stocks	30 Years	100%	100%	100%	99%	97%	94%	91%	86%	82%
	40 Years	100%	100%	99%	97%	93%	88%	84%	80%	76%
	50 Years	100%	100%	99%	95%	90%	85%	81%	77%	73%
	60 Years	100%	99%	98%	94%	89%	84%	80%	75%	70%
75% Stocks	30 Years	100%	100%	100%	100%	99%	95%	90%	84%	80%
	40 Years	100%	100%	100%	98%	93%	86%	82%	76%	69%
	50 Years	100%	100%	99%	94%	88%	82%	76%	69%	62%
	60 Years	100%	100%	97%	92%	85%	80%	71%	65%	58%
50% Stocks	30 Years	100%	100%	100%	100%	95%	91%	85%	77%	70%
	40 Years	100%	100%	98%	93%	86%	76%	65%	59%	51%
	50 Years	100%	98%	93%	85%	74%	63%	55%	46%	41%
	60 Years	100%	96%	89%	79%	65%	57%	48%	42%	36%
25% Stocks	30 Years	100%	100%	98%	90%	80%	70%	63%	57%	51%
	40 Years	97%	89%	77%	64%	55%	47%	37%	34%	32%
	50 Years	85%	75%	62%	51%	40%	34%	31%	29%	23%
	60 Years	78%	65%	51%	39%	33%	31%	27%	21%	17%
0% Stocks	30 Years	89%	80%	68%	61%	54%	50%	45%	40%	34%
	40 Years	64%	56%	47%	39%	33%	29%	24%	21%	18%
	50 Years	50%	39%	31%	27%	23%	19%	14%	12%	9%
	60 Years	35%	30%	25%	22%	16%	12%	9%	7%	7%

Source: Early Retirement Now

Jack's eyes swam all over the sheet. "Where am I even supposed to look?"

"First, look at the 5% withdrawal rate for a 50% stock portfolio over a 40-year retirement."

"Okay…"

"What's the percentage likelihood you'd make it to life expectancy without running out of money?"

Jack traced his hand along the X-axis of the chart. "Looks like 51%."

"Are those odds you could live with?"

"Not a chance!"

"Is there a rate of withdrawal with which you would feel comfortable?"

He studied the chart for a moment. "Well, it says here that if I had a 50% stock portfolio, and I only withdrew 4% of my portfolio per year over a 40-year retirement, I'd have an 86% chance of never running out of money. I could live with those odds."

"Most people can. In fact, the 4% distribution rate has become the gold standard in our industry. You take out more than 4% in a given year and you're really rolling the dice."

Jack frowned for a moment as he let the information sink in. Then he snatched up his laptop and began typing.

"If what you're saying is true," he said, "then a 4% distribution rate, or $120,000 per year, should have saved my stepfather."

He changed the annual cash flow on his calculator, hit enter, and watched the results flash onto his screen.

Year	Beginning of Year Account Value	Earnings Rate	Annual Cash Cash Flow	End of Year Account Value
2000	$3,000,000	-9.17%	-$120,000	$2,615,904
2001	$2,615,904	-11.72%	-$120,000	$2,203,384
2002	$2,203,384	-24.02%	-$120,000	$1,582,955
2003	$1,582,955	28.82%	-$120,000	$1,884,579
2004	$1,884,579	11.73%	-$120,000	$1,971,564
2005	$1,971,564	5.23%	$120,000	$1,948,401
2006	$1,948,401	15.62%	-$120,000	$2,113,997
2007	$2,113,997	4.87%	-$120,000	$2,091,105
2008	$2,091,105	-39.05%	-$120,000	$1,201,388
2009	$1,201,388	26.52%	-$120,000	$1,368,172
2010	$1,368,172	15.12%	-$120,000	$1,436,896
2011	$1,436,896	2.03%	-$120,000	$1,343,629
2012	$1,343,629	17.11%	-$120,000	$1,432,992
2013	$1,432,992	35.33%	-$120,000	$1,776,872

Year	Beginning of Year Account Value	Earnings Rate	Annual Cash Cash Flow	End of Year Account Value
2014	$1,776,872	19.13%	-$120,000	$1,973,832
2015	$1,973,832	15.84%	-$120,000	$2,147,479
2016	$2,147,479	19.21%	-$120,000	$2,416,957
2017	$2,416,957	31.41%	-$120,000	$3,018,432
2018	$3,018,432	-10.18%	-$120,000	$2,603,371

"Unbelievable. If he'd begun with a 4% withdrawal rate, he'd still have over $2.6 million left, even after those three down years at the outset."

Jane's approval deepened. "Now you're getting it."

And that's when it hit Jack. He pulled out his smartphone and did a quick calculation.

"At $165,000 per year, my stepfather was withdrawing 5.5% of his portfolio." Jack once again traced his finger across the chart. "At 5.5% withdrawals, he's off the chart! He didn't even have a 50% shot of his money lasting until life expectancy!"

"You can start to see why average rates of return are so misleading," Jane pointed out.

"Okay, so I think I'm with you," Jack said. "But what if he hadn't retired during those three down years? What if he had retired in a period of relative prosperity and growing markets?"

"Then things might have been different," Jane said. "May I see your laptop again so that I can illustrate my point?"

"By all means." Jack slid the laptop across the desk.

Jane grabbed the sheet of Ted's returns and began typing on the keyboard. After a few minutes she hit the enter key.

"Voila! I reversed the order of the rates of return. In this scenario, your stepfather would have only had one down year in his first ten, and then finished with those three down years. Look at where that puts him by 2018."

Year	Beginning of Year Account Value	Earnings Rate	Annual Cash Cash Flow	End of Year Account Value
2000	$3,000,000	-10.18%	-$165,000	$2,546,397
2001	$2,546,397	31.41%	-$165,000	$3,129,394
2002	$3,129,394	19.21%	-$165,000	$3,533,854
2003	$3,533,854	15.84%	-$165,000	$3,902,480
2004	$3,902,480	19.13%	-$165,000	$4,452,460
2005	$4,452,460	35.33%	-$165,000	$5,802,220
2006	$5,802,220	17.11%	-$165,000	$6,601,748
2007	$6,601,748	2.03%	-$165,000	$6,567,414
2008	$6,567,414	15.12%	-$165,000	$7,370,459
2009	$7,370,459	26.52%	-$165,000	$9,116,347
2010	$9,116,347	-39.05%	-$165,000	$5,455,846
2011	$5,455,846	4.87%	-$165,000	$5,548,510
2012	$5,548,510	15.62%	-$165,000	$6,224,415
2013	$6,224,415	5.23%	-$165,000	$6,376,322
2014	$6,376,322	11.73%	-$165,000	$6,939,910
2015	$6,939,910	28.82%	-$165,000	$8,727,439
2016	$8,727,439	-24.02%	-$165,000	$6,505,741
2017	$6,505,741	-11.72%	-$165,000	$5,597,606
2018	$5,597,606	-9.17%	-$165,000	$4,934,436

Jack looked over the new set of numbers. "He never runs out of money, even at 5.5% withdrawal rates."

"And he has $4.9 million left over at the end," Jane added.

"What does all this mean? That my stepfather just got incredibly unlucky?"

"That's part of it, to be sure. But the broader point is this: you never know what the rates of return are going to be in your first year of retirement. Or your second. Or your third. You don't know if you'll have two down years in the first ten years or four. If you're drawing out more than 4%, and happen to retire in the wrong year, then you could unwittingly exhaust your portfolio 15 years earlier than you thought. Or 25 years earlier for that matter. That's why the 4% rule is sacrosanct."

Jack stewed in his chair as he considered the implications of Bruce Lassiter's laissez-faire financial management. Sure, he'd helped Ted achieve a robust *average* annual rate of return, but Jack was now seeing that there was so much more to the equation than that. How could Bruce have permitted Ted to withdraw 5.5% *every year?*

"So, it's a minor miracle he has anything left at this point?" Jack asked.

"This *is* bad, Mr. Wheeler, but it could have been much, *much* worse."

"How could my stepfather's advisor have allowed this to happen?" Jack asked indignantly.

"Because he failed to realize one of the most important axioms in retirement planning. The goal is not just to accumulate a lot of money. Or get to the top of the mountain, as we like to say. The real goal is to get to the top of the mountain, then get back down again safely. That means building a nest egg *and* making sure it lasts until death. That's why the 4% rule is so important. And with that," she said, rising to her feet, "I'm afraid our time has come to an end."

Jane's discussion on withdrawal rates and sequence of return risk wasn't the answer Jack had been looking for, but it had given him insight into Bruce Lassiter's approach to retirement planning. Now he had all the evidence he needed to confront Bruce in person.

"Do you mind if I come back tomorrow? I have a few more questions."

"See Heather on your way out. I might have 20 minutes where I can squeeze you in."

His first meeting with Jane had been incredibly enlightening, and he was looking forward to plying her with more questions. But first, it was time to confront Bruce Lassiter. And he knew exactly how he would do it.

CHAPTER 6

Jack sat in his car outside of Bruce Lassiter's office as he waited for the lunch hour to approach. After another set of failed attempts to reach Bruce by phone and in person, Jack had decided to surveil Bruce's office from the safety of his rental car. And so, he waited, watching the front door of the office where no one could enter or exit without his noticing.

It was just past noon when Bruce finally emerged and began walking briskly down the street. Jack hopped out of his car and began following from a distance. He proceeded cautiously, keeping his head down, glancing only occasionally in Bruce's direction. After a few blocks, Bruce broke off and ducked into a diner.

When Jack reached the diner, he stepped in and began scanning the tables. Bruce had been seated at a booth by the front window. It was the perfect placement. If Bruce started to make a scene, it would draw attention from the other customers as well as any passersby in the street. Jack walked over to the table and slid onto the bench across from the Bruce.

"Hello, Bruce."

Startled, Bruce put down his menu. "Do I know you?"

"You know my stepfather, Ted Hardy."

Bruce quickly conjured up a manufactured smile and extended his hand across the table. "So terribly sorry to hear about Ted. It's just a tragedy."

Jack ignored his hand. "You've been busy, Bruce. If I didn't know any better, I'd say you've been avoiding me."

"Not at all," Bruce said with a dismissive laugh. "I apologize that I haven't been able to meet with you. We've been drowning in meetings and paperwork lately and, I'll have you know, your stepfather's a big part of that. When the Legend of Lancaster is one of your clients, it's like a having a walking billboard."

"If Ted is so important to your practice, I'm surprised you let him go broke. You sat by and watched for 19 years as his distributions far exceeded what his portfolio could sustain. After starting off his retirement with three straight down years, you should've said something, you should've intervened. Why didn't you?"

Bruce dropped all the pretenses and raised an angry finger up to Jack's face. "I don't see how you're fit to lecture *me* on how to do *my* job. We maximize our clients' rates of return with as little risk as possible. I'll stack my average annual returns up against anyone else's out there."

"I'm not questioning your average annual returns Bruce. I just can't figure out why you'd advocate taking annual withdrawals of 5.5% on a portfolio that needed to last at least 35 years. You *knew* that withdrawal rate was too aggressive, yet you did nothing. Even worse, you told Ted to 'set it and forget it.' And now, he'll be broke within the year."

Bruce shook his head. "You're confusing me with a financial planner. Clients come to me because of my high average annual rates of return. What they do with their money is their business."

"But I saw the projection you provided for Ted 19 years ago. It showed 9% growth and $165,000 annual distributions."

"Of course. Because those are the numbers *he* gave *me*. I had a paraplanner feed those numbers into the software and spit out a report. But that was only because Ted wanted some sort of a written plan. Retirement planning is not what I do. Take a look at my website and see if you can find those words anywhere on there. I grow my clients' money. That's it. End of story."

"But how could you have let the last ten years go by while Ted spent his portfolio into oblivion? Didn't his withdrawal rate ever come up in your annual reviews?"

Bruce glared at Jack before the anger suddenly drained from his face. He paused for a long moment before speaking. "Ted hasn't stepped foot in my office since 2008. Since just after your mom passed."

Jack's eyes narrowed with suspicion. "Impossible. Ted was obsessed with the idea of a worry-free retirement. Wouldn't ever shut up about it. There's no way he'd stop talking to the guy who was keeping tabs on his portfolio, especially if he was running out of cash!"

"A lot happened after your mom's passing. Ted started to let go. He stopped coming to our annual reviews. He stopped responding to my phone calls. He even avoided me when our paths crossed in public. And all the while, he kept taking those $165,000 annual distributions. It's like he didn't care if he ran out of money."

Jack sat there, searching for words. What Bruce was describing didn't sound like Ted at all. Ted would never have simply thrown open the purse strings and let it rip. It wasn't in his nature. But then again, there *had* been a lot of unopened investment statements in Ted's file as well as the lapsed term policy. Could Genevieve's death have been enough to sap the zeal from his life? Had Ted simply let go and spent himself into oblivion?

Jack had walked into the diner convinced that Bruce Lassiter was the main culprit in the collapse of Ted's finances. Now he wasn't so sure. If Bruce was telling the truth, Ted's unfettered spending in the wake of his wife's death had been his ruin. Either way, Jack needed to gather more clues.

* * *

"So, how goes the financial power of attorney business?" Annie asked as Jack settled into an overstuffed chair in her living room.

"Not very well, I'm afraid."

Annie's brow creased with concern. "What do you mean? All you have to do is go over to Sunset and set up some sort of automatic deduction, right? You should be on a plane back to California by tomorrow morning."

"I wish it were that simple, Annie. There's no easy way to put this, so I'm just going to come right out with it: Ted has $71,000 to his name."

Annie shook her head. "That can't be right."

"I'm afraid it is," Jack said. "Apparently, Ted thought it was a good idea to take $165,000 distributions like clockwork, regardless of market conditions. Even after Mom died, he just kept on spending that $165,000."

"But Bruce *did* get him a reasonable average rate of return, didn't he?"

"More than reasonable," Jack acknowledged. "But none of that matters once you hit retirement. Once you start withdrawing money, it's the order in which those returns are received that makes all the difference. Ted and Mom retired at the worst possible time. Their first three years of retirement were all under water. The combination of market loss and consistent $165,000 annual distributions sent their portfolio into a tailspin from which it never recovered."

The confusion in Annie's eyes began to give way to fear. "So, what—what does all this mean?"

"It means that, unless you have a pile of money earmarked for Ted's long-term care expenses, he'll be living out the rest of his days at St. Luke's over on Fifth."

She shuddered as the tears brimmed at the corners of her eyes and then spilled over.

"Can I ask you a question, Annie?" Jack said. He had come over to break the bad news, but there was one other detail he'd hoped to ferret out.

She nodded. "Of course."

"After Mom died, did Ted seem like he was letting go?"

"What do you mean?"

"You know, lost his zeal for life. Stopped caring. Started spending money in a willy-nilly way?"

Annie dabbed at her tears, then shook her head. "He definitely changed after Mom died, but not in the way you're suggesting. No lavish trips or new cars if that's what you mean. Why do you ask?"

"I've been digging around and noticed a few things. After Mom died, it looks like he paid less attention to his finances." Jack explained about the missed annual reviews, the unreturned phone calls to Bruce Lassiter, the lapsed insurance policy, and the consistent $165,000 distributions regardless of market conditions.

"You're right, that doesn't seem like Dad at all. Could he really have spent his entire fortune down to nothing?"

"I can't say for sure," Jack said darkly. "But the evidence is piling up."

CHAPTER 7

The next morning, Jack began to synthesize all the bits of data that had taken up residence in his brain. What Jane had taught him had blown his financial paradigm to pieces. She'd exposed the reckless practice of relying on high average rates of return during retirement. She'd also introduced an entirely new principle that had given Jack serious pause: the 4% rule.

As Jack sat at the breakfast table in Ted's condo, he pulled up his 401(k) account on his phone and stared at the balance. $230,321. If he retired today, the most he could safely withdraw from his account would be $9,200. A pittance. Hardly worth mentioning. The longer he stared at the number, the more his spirits waned. Then a nightmarish thought settled over him. If constrained by the 4% rule, he'd need a massive amount of money to meet his $100,000 annual lifestyle need in retirement. He did a quick calculation and gulped when he saw the number.

$2,500,000.

In order to generate the income he required in retirement, he'd need to accumulate an additional $2,270,000 in 20 short years. To come up with the savings required to reach that number, he'd have to downsize his house, downgrade both cars, and swap vacations for modest weekend getaways. It was that, or risk spending his waning years in a Medicaid-funded facility like Ted. And that was an alternative he refused to accept.

* * *

"You look terrible," Jane said as she looked across her desk at Jack.

"Thanks," Jack said sullenly.

"What's on your mind?"

Jack took a deep breath before beginning. "Our conversation yesterday got me thinking about my own retirement. If I can never take more than 4% of my initial starting balance in retirement, then I'm going to need a massive account balance if I *ever* hope to retire."

"Massive is all relative. Tell me what that word means to you."

"If I wanted $100,000 per year in retirement, excluding Social Security, I'd have to save up $2,500,000 in the next 20 years."

"Ah, you've discovered the dark underbelly of the 4% rule. The lower your distribution rate in retirement, the larger the nest egg required to meet your lifestyle needs. If you don't mind me asking, how much money do you currently have in your retirement accounts?"

Jack's answer was imbued with despair. "Only about $230,000 in my 401(k). There's no way I'll get there in 20 years. It's a bridge too far."

"It's not *entirely* hopeless, Mr. Wheeler. Give me a second here." She pulled out a financial calculator and began inputting numbers. "What's a realistic rate of return, net of fees?"

"I don't know anymore. Seven percent, I guess?"

"Not unreasonable in today's environment. And how much are you currently saving?"

"I contribute the full $19,000 to my 401(k).

"Any match?"

"Dollar for dollar up to three percent of my income."

"And how much do you make?"

"$150,000."

"And how old are you now?"

"I'm 45."

"Retire at 65?"

"That's right."

She tapped a few more buttons on her calculator, then turned it in Jack's direction. "Based on my quick calculations, you're going to be about $650,000 short."

Jack felt a wave of panic wash over him. This was exactly what he'd been afraid of. "How do I bridge the gap? What are my options?"

"With a retirement shortfall like yours, you have five options. The most obvious one is this: you need to save more money. Given your retirement objectives, you're just not saving enough."

"How much more would I have to save?" he asked, bracing for the response.

Jane hit a few keys. "About $16,000 per year."

Jack winced.

"I don't know, Jane. Every single dime in my budget is accounted for. What's the second option?"

"So, you're *not* willing to save more money?"

"I don't see how I could. Certainly not another $16,000 per year."

"All right. Then there's option two: you can work longer. Instead of working until 65, give your retirement accounts the chance to grow and compound a little bit longer."

"How much longer?"

Another quick calculation.

"Four years longer. You'd only be 69. That's not so bad!"

"I think I'll pass," Jack said with a grimace. "I *really* don't want to work any longer than I absolutely have to."

"Option number three: you can die sooner," she said with a playful wink.

"Ha ha," Jack said. "I appreciate your willingness to be so light-hearted about my life expectancy, but I think I'll pass on that, too. Next option?"

"Option number four: you can spend less in retirement. Based on your current savings level, you'll have a little over $1.85 million at retirement. With the 4% rule, you'd be able to spend $74,000 per year. Would that work for you?"

"With the type of retirement that my wife and I envision, I just don't think $74,000 will be enough."

"Given the questionable future of Social Security," she said, "$74,000 may be all you can expect."

"This keeps getting better and better," Jack said dryly. "What's the next alternative?"

"Option number five: take more risk in the stock market."

"You mean try for a higher rate of return?"

Jane nodded as she did another calculation. She cringed when she saw the result. "You'd need to grow your money at 9% instead of 7%."

"But to pull that off," Jack said, "I'd have to take a *lot* more risk in the market, right?"

"That's true," Jane agreed. "As a rule of thumb, a 45-year-old like you should only have 55% of his portfolio allocated to stocks. To get a 9% rate of return, that number would need to go higher."

"But taking more risk doesn't guarantee a higher return, right?"

"Unfortunately not. If ratcheting up the risk of a portfolio were a silver bullet, everyone would be doing it. More risk means wider swings in the market which means that, in theory, you could miss your retirement goals by an even wider margin."

Jack's vision for a fully-funded, care-free, set-it-and-forget-it retirement was evaporating before his eyes.

"To recap," Jack said, "I can either save more, spend less, work longer, die sooner, or take more risk in the stock market. But with that last option, I could, in theory, run out of money even faster."

Jane gave him a rueful smile. "Truth be told, the first four options don't have any guarantees either, because they all depend on that 7% rate of return."

"Wow," Jack said dejectedly. "And you're *sure* there isn't some magical sixth option that's not quite as painful?" Jack asked, a pleading look in his eyes.

Jane's smile faded. She drew quiet and solemn, fixing him with a stare that seemed to penetrate deep into his soul. After a few moments she finally answered, "I'm sorry, Mr. Wheeler; I'm afraid there are no other options."

CHAPTER 8

As Jack walked out to his car, he replayed that final exchange over again in his mind. *I'm sorry, Mr. Wheeler; I'm afraid there are no other options.* Before she'd handed down her grim verdict, Jane had seemed to be studying him, almost weighing him in the balance. Either there were *only* five solutions for his problem or there were more than five. Why had she delayed her response?

As Jane's words pinged around in his brain, a familiar figure approached from the sidewalk in front of Jane's building. Sal Giordano. He was the last person Jack wanted to see right now. All he needed was for Sal to uncover the real state of Ted's financial situation, and then splash it all over the local papers. No one deserved to have their personal financial failings exposed to the world. Not even Ted.

"Hello, Jack. What brings you to this part of town?" Sal asked. He had an unctuous quality to him that left Jack unsettled.

"Private business," Jack said, fishing out his keys.

"You know, Jack, it's no secret that Bruce Lassiter handles Ted's finances. And I have to say, you looked a little distressed when you walked out of his office yesterday."

"What are you, spying on me?" Jack asked incredulously.

Sal swatted Jack's question aside and plowed ahead. "Now I catch you on the other side of town, walking out of Jane Fletcher's office. There really are only two options as I see it. First, Ted moved some assets over to Jane and you're just here to wrap up loose ends. Doesn't seem likely since Bruce Lassiter would move heaven and earth to keep Ted as his client. Second, and this is the more likely scenario, Ted's finances aren't quite what you thought they were. You're here at Fletcher Financial to get a second opinion, figure out exactly what went wrong. Am I right?"

The ease with which Sal had pieced this together sent a chill down Jack's spine. He couldn't get out of there fast enough. But Sal wasn't done.

"Still no comment, huh? Well, rest assured, Mr. Wheeler, I'm hot on the trail and the clues are starting to pile up. I happen to believe that Ted Hardy has much less money than one would expect of a retired NFL quarterback and successful businessman. If he really did burn through his fortune in the short span of 19 years...why, that'd make quite the story. Quite the story indeed."

Jack refused to rise to the bait. He knew better than to give Sal Giordano any more information than he already had.

"Good bye, Mr. Giordano. A distinct pleasure. As usual."

*   *   *

As Jack drove home, the revelations brought out during his meeting with Jane Fletcher began to paralyze him with dread. For starters, Ted's financial condition virtually guaranteed he'd be spending the last few years of his life wasting away in a Medicaid-funded long-term care facility. Despite Ted's many failings, he didn't deserve to live out his final chapter in those conditions.

Furthermore, it was becoming increasingly clear that, short of a miracle, there was no way he was going to hit his own retirement goals. The five alternatives laid out by Jane all required sacrifices he wasn't prepared to make. All this because of a mysterious financial planning principle known as sequence of return risk. If his distributions in retirement exceeded 4%, there was a high likelihood he could end up broke, wasting away in a Medicaid-funded facility, just like Ted.

These two stress points danced around in his mind, mingling with a third source of angst. He was convinced that Jane was holding out on him. If there were only five alternatives to bridge his retirement shortfall, why the long, thoughtful pause before saying so? Why did she seem to be weighing him in the balance? *Was* there a sixth choice? If so, had she found him unworthy of it? As he stewed over this possibility, his mood turned sour and then dark.

Of one thing Jack *was* certain: if there was a sixth, less-painful alternative, he was going to find out what it was.

CHAPTER 9

"Mr. Wheeler," Jane said, looking up from her lunch. "I wasn't aware we had another appointment."

"We don't, and I apologize for the intrusion. I'm just feeling a bit unsettled about the way our conversation ended yesterday."

Jane glanced at the clock on the wall behind him. "I have ten minutes before my next appointment."

With no time to waste, he launched right in. "When you told me there were only five options to solve my retirement shortfall, I got the sense you were holding something back. It's been bothering me ever since. So, level with me, Jane: *is* there another strategy you're not telling me about? A sixth way, if you will?"

Jane fixed him with another long, cryptic stare. Jack met her with his own steady gaze. He knew that in these sorts of standoffs, the one who spoke first was the one who usually lost. He wasn't going to back down. Not now.

After a long moment of silence, Jane finally spoke. "There is, in fact, another alternative. A sixth way, as you put it."

"I knew it!"

"But, I don't think it's right for you," Jane said in the next breath. "Now, if you don't mind, I have to prepare for my next appointment."

Jack felt his burgeoning hope burst like a balloon.

"Wha…what do you mean it's not right for me? It *has* to be right for me. My current savings plan is woefully underfunded. None of the first five options you listed will work. The stars are aligned for the sixth way. I'm the perfect candidate!"

Jane shook her head. "I don't want to go down this road with you, Mr. Wheeler. I've encountered your type before. I've waged the battles. And in the end, it always ends up being an exercise in futility. I'm too busy, and there are too many other people who *are* willing to do what I tell them. Now if you'll excuse me, I have a client to meet with."

"What do I have to do to convince you that I want your help?" Jack asked, the panic rising in his voice. "Do I have to get on my knees and beg? I don't want to end up like my stepfather. I swear I'll be the perfect student. I'll pay attention. I'll do my homework assignments. I'll do *everything* you ask of me."

As Jane continued to sit there in silence, his hopes began to wane. His chin fell to his chest as he turned to leave.

"Not so fast, Mr. Wheeler," Jane called to him. She gestured for him to take a seat across from her.

Surprised, Jack walked over to the chair and fell into it.

"I'll help you, but I have conditions."

Jack slid forward to the very edge of his seat. "Anything," he pleaded. "I'll do anything."

"I *will* share the sixth strategy. But I have to warn you, it involves concepts that will challenge your financial worldview. I'm open to a debate, but if you don't put your ego on the shelf, I'm done. Your adherence to the traditional paradigms is what got you into this mess. If I sense that you're too blinded by conventional wisdom or whatever you read online last week, you can take your 4% withdrawal rate and hit the road."

Jack nodded and swallowed hard. He still couldn't figure out how he'd crossed her, but he wasn't about to miss out on this opportunity.

"I have a brief opening tomorrow morning at 9 a.m. Don't be late."

CHAPTER 10

Jack showed up at Jane's office the next morning at 8:55 a.m. By 9 a.m., they had begun.

"If you could pin the failure of your stepfather's plan on just one thing, what would it be?" Jane asked.

"He took out more than 4% per year," Jack said reflexively. If there was one recurring theme so far, this was it.

"And why was that such a fatal mistake?"

"When you take out more than 4% on a prolonged basis, your assets can't sustain it."

"And why can't they sustain it?"

Jack thought about it for a moment. "When you take a distribution during a down year, you kill off the worker dollars that are supposed to be earning you money."

"That's right. So, the question becomes, how iron-clad is that 4% rule? Are there any scenarios where you could take out more than 4%? How about 7%? How about 10%?"

Jack felt a thrill of excitement shoot through him. This was exactly what he was hoping for. If he could somehow shed the shackles of that onerous 4% rule, he could easily bridge his retirement shortfall.

"How could that work?" Jack asked eagerly. "What you're describing flies in the face of all the studies you cited earlier. The Monte Carlo scenarios don't work out. If I take out 5%, the likelihood of my investments lasting until life expectancy drops down to 50%. I can't imagine what 7% would do."

"Do you still have your stepfather's spreadsheet handy?

Jack nodded, pulling his laptop out of his bag.

"Here's what I want you to do," Jane said. "For every down year in the first ten years, I want you to modify the spreadsheet. Instead of showing your stepfather taking out $165,000 in those down years, I want you to simply show a zero. No withdrawals at all."

Jack frowned. He wasn't sure why eliminating withdrawals in the down years was going to show anything other than the obvious—more money at the end. Ted couldn't have just lived off top ramen during those down years. What would this prove?

"Okay, give me a second."

"Well?" Jane asked once he'd finished typing. "What can you tell me?"

Year	Beginning of Year Account Value	Earnings Rate	Annual Cash Cash Flow	End of Year Account Value
2000	$3,000,000	-9.17%	$0	$2,724,900
2001	$2,724,900	-11.72%	$0	$2,405,542
2002	$2,405,542	-24.02%	$0	$1,827,731
2003	$1,827,731	28.82%	-$165,000	$2,141,930
2004	$2,141,930	11.73%	-$165,000	$2,208,823
2005	$2,208,823	5.23%	-$165,000	$2,150,715
2006	$2,150,715	15.62%	-$165,000	$2,295,884
2007	$2,295,884	4.87%	-$165,000	$2,234,658
2008	$2,234,658	-39.05%	$0	$1,362,024

Year	Beginning of Year Account Value	Earnings Rate	Annual Cash Cash Flow	End of Year Account Value
2009	$1,362,024	26.52%	-$165,000	$1,514,475
2010	$1,514,475	15.12%	-$165,000	$1,553,516
2011	$1,553,516	2.03%	-$165,000	$1,416,702
2012	$1,416,702	17.11%	-$165,000	$1,465,869
2013	$1,465,869	35.33%	-$165,000	$1,760,466
2014	$1,760,466	19.13%	-$165,000	$1,900,678
2015	$1,900,678	15.84%	-$165,000	$2,010,610
2016	$2,010,610	19.21%	-$165,000	$2,200,151
2017	$2,200,151	31.41%	-$165,000	$2,674,392
2018	$2,674,392	10.18%	-$165,000	$2,253,936

"My stepfather would currently be sitting on over $2 million in his investments. Surprising, but not *that* surprising." Jack shook his head in protest. "There's only one problem: how could you *not* take distributions from your portfolios during the down years?"

Jane flashed him another approving smile. "Now you're starting to see the problem, Mr. Wheeler. In order to avoid taking distributions from a volatile stock market portfolio in retirement, you have to have a *separate* account from which to take distributions. For our purposes, we'll call this account the volatility shield."

"Volatility shield?" Jack asked. He hadn't heard the term before.

"That's right. It's an account that's earmarked specifically for lifestyle expenses during any down years in your first ten years of retirement."

"Why only the first ten years?"

"The Monte Carlo simulations show that in a typical 25-year retirement, the first ten years are the most crucial. If you can avoid taking distributions from your stock market portfolio during the down years in those first ten years, then there's very little risk of running out of money in the remaining 15."

"I see," Jack said, intrigued. "Go on."

"Now, not just any old account will do. A volatility shield must possess a number of specific attributes if it's going to truly protect you from volatility. Here's the first ground rule: it must be guaranteed to never lose money. An investment can't shield your financial world from volatility if it's riding the stock market roller coaster."

"Okay, that makes sense. To pay for lifestyle expenses during those down years, the account can't be underwater. You need to be able to rely upon that bucket of money, even if the stock market is tanking."

"That's exactly right," Jane said. "The volatility shield has to be immune from stock market volatility. It has to be 100% safe."

"So, like a savings account?"

"Nice thought, but no. While savings accounts are safe, they lack another critical quality. And that leads us to ground rule two: a volatility shield must be productive. And while savings accounts *do* have guarantees against loss, most won't even keep up with inflation."

"So a volatility shield has to be 100% safe *and* productive, all at the same time?"

"You got it."

"How, exactly, are you defining productive?"

"Between 4% and 6% over time."

"Four percent to 6%?"

"Over time," Jane reminded him.

"Okay, 4% to 6% *over time*. But what you're describing is an oxymoron. Return is a function of risk. No risk, no reward. What kind of investment could possibly give you productive growth with no risk?

"Patience, Mr. Wheeler. When I'm done defining the volatility shield's required attributes, I'll let you know about the investment vehicle itself. We can cover the other ground rules tomorrow morning. For today, I'm out of time."

"How many ground rules are we going to cover?" Jack pressed. "I've already been in town a lot longer than I thought I'd be and…"

Jane gave him a withering look that seemed to say, *We're going to do this on my time frame, or we aren't going to do it at all.*

Jack's hands came up in a gesture of surrender. "I got it. I got it. What time?"

"I can squeeze you in for a few minutes at 10:30 tomorrow morning. Don't be late."

CHAPTER 11

Nerves and excitement roiled within Jack as he stepped into Jane's office the next morning.

"Thanks for squeezing me in," Jack said as he slid into the chair across from Jane.

"You have 15 minutes today," she told him. "And then I have another appointment."

Jack chafed in his chair. At this rate, he was going to be here for another week before learning the true identity of the volatility shield. But her earlier warnings kept his protests in check.

"I'm grateful for whatever time you can spare," he said, forcing a smile.

"Good. To begin, I'd like you to recite the first two ground rules of the volatility shield accompanied by an explanation of each."

Jack swallowed hard. He hadn't expected to be quizzed on the information so quickly. "Uh, right. First rule of a volatility shield: no market loss. The whole point of a volatility shield is to provide for your living expenses in a down market so that your assets have the chance to recover. If your volatility shield tanks right along with the market, then it can't perform its stated purpose. Ground rule two: your volatility shield must grow productively."

"And why is that?" Jane prodded.

"Well, to be honest, that's what I'm having a hard time with. I thought about it all last night. Why *does* your volatility shield need to be productive? Let's say you can fully fund your volatility shield by the time you retire. Aren't you planning on just spending it during those first ten years anyway? And if you are planning on spending it during those first ten years, who cares if it grows productively or not?"

Jack held his breath, bracing for Jane's response. She'd said she was open to debate, but if he came across as too brash, he might be out on his ear.

"That's a good question, Mr. Wheeler," she said after a pause.

Jack's breath released.

"And it's a perfect segue into ground rule three: your volatility shield must be in place *before* you reach retirement."

Jack puzzled over that for a second before finally asking, "Why's that?"

"Because it's impossible to know when the market will drop. It could happen the very first year of your retirement. In your stepfather's case, it was the first *three* years of retirement."

"If it needs to be in place at retirement," Jack said, "then you'd have to start funding this thing years in advance."

"That's true. The fastest I've ever seen anyone fully fund their volatility shield is four years. For most people, it's going to take ten years or more. You can start to see why this isn't an appropriate strategy for someone who wants to retire tomorrow. By that point, it's too late."

"I think I understand," Jack said, nodding slowly.

"Good. Now that you understand ground rule three, we can circle back to your question about ground rule two."

"Why volatility shields need to be productive."

She nodded. "Let's say that you need at least three years' worth of living expenses in your volatility shield by the time you retire."

"Okay."

"Let's also say that you begin funding your account 20 years before your anticipated retirement date. What would happen to the size of your contributions if you didn't have the luxury of growing them productively over that 20-year time frame?"

"They'd have to be a whole lot bigger."

"That's exactly right. Find an investment that grows safely *and* productively, and you won't have to fund it as aggressively."

"That makes a lot of sense."

"There's one other thing, Mr. Wheeler."

"Shoot."

"What if you *were* lucky enough to pass through the first ten years of retirement with only one or two down years?"

Jack thought about it for a moment. "Then you'd still have some money left over at the beginning of the eleventh year. So, any unused funds in the volatility shield would continue to grow—"

"Safely and productively," Jane said, finishing his sentence.

"Okay, let's see if I can summarize," Jack offered. "The third ground rule of the volatility shield is that it must be fully funded *before* you reach retirement. For most people, this could take ten years or longer. And, if the money within your volatility shield can grow safely and productively, then you won't have to contribute nearly as much. Lastly, if there's money left over at the end of those first ten years of retirement, it still needs to grow safely and productively."

"Couldn't have said it better myself," Jane beamed.

Jack couldn't help but grin. "I think I'm ready!"

"Ready for what?" Jane asked, the smile fading from her face.

"To learn about which investment qualifies as a volatility shield."

Jane gave him a long, stern look, and Jack receded into his chair.

"I'm not going to reveal the identity of the volatility shield right now, because I haven't laid out the fourth and, perhaps, most important ground rule."

Jack shifted restlessly. How much longer was she going to drag this thing out?

"All right," he said, a touch of frustration in his voice. "Lay it on me."

"I would love to, Mr. Wheeler. But I'm afraid our 15 minutes are up. Be in my office tomorrow morning again at 9 a.m. sharp. And don't dilly dally. I won't have a lot of time."

CHAPTER 12

As Jack approached highway 32 the next morning, rush hour traffic had already backed up onto the onramp. Fearful of being late for his appointment, he took a shortcut through town. As he pulled onto Newton Street just inside the city limits, a familiar structure rose up on his right: the Lancaster Boys Club. Though it was a far cry from what he remembered 19 years earlier. Nearly every window in the building was broken and tall weeds sprouted from the mapwork of cracks in the parking lot. The exterior of the building was faded and the once prominent sign was now missing. It looked like it hadn't been open in years. Clearly, Mel hadn't garnered the funds necessary to keep the doors open. Jack wondered about the lives that had been ruined by the center's closing. He felt a spark of anger as he remembered Ted's flippant response to his request for help that day.

By the time Jack made it to Fletcher Financial five minutes later, only one thought could buoy his spirits: he was one day closer to knowing the identity of the volatility shield.

He checked in with Heather at the front desk, and, within a few moments, was ushered into Jane's office.

"Good morning, Mr. Wheeler," Jane said, a fresh smile on her face. "You doing all right? You look a little down."

"Sorry if I seem out of sorts. I just drove past the old Lancaster Boys Club over on Newton. That place really saved me when it was just me and my mom. Sad to see it so rundown."

"Ah, yes, Mel Kauffman had to shut it down about 18 years ago. He's been directing the soup kitchen over on Main ever since."

Jack frowned at this revelation.

"Anyway, time is short. Shall we get down to business?" Jane asked.

"Absolutely. I'm anxious to learn about ground rule four."

"Before we get to that," she said, "we need to lay a little groundwork first. Have you ever heard about a man named David Walker?"

Jack shook his head. "Can't say that I have."

"I'm not surprised. The most important people in our country are usually the least heralded. David Walker is one of those people. He was the Comptroller General of the Federal Government. He served in that position for ten years, first under President Clinton and then under President Bush. He was basically the CPA of the USA. He knows more about the fiscal condition of our great country than just about anyone else on the planet."

"Impressive credentials," Jack said.

"In 2010, he went on NPR and told millions of listeners that there would come a time in our country when tax rates would have to double."

"Double?" Jack asked, eyes widening.

"*Double.* He then challenged the radio show hostess to come up with a four-letter word that would explain why. Well, she couldn't figure out what it was, so they opened up the phone lines and people started to call in, offering their best four-letter guesses."

"Debt?" Jack ventured.

"That was the most popular guess, and certainly that's part of the equation, but it doesn't tell the whole story. Other answers included wars, jobs, and kids. One guy even said health."

Jack chuckled.

"But, in the end," Jane continued, "nobody could figure out what that four-letter word was."

"What was the answer?"

"Math."

"Math?" Jack said, confused. "What did he mean by math?"

"Math is the dirty little secret that nobody in Washington wants to talk about. David Walker said that to deliver on all of the entitlement programs like Social Security, Medicare, and Medicaid, we'd have to double taxes immediately. Now, we don't *have* to double tax rates immediately, but for every year we postpone doubling taxes, the national debt will grow by $2 trillion, on average, each and every year until we hit this magical moment in our country when we have $53 trillion of debt. Do you know why that's a significant number, Jack?"

"I don't."

"If we had $53 trillion of debt, then all of the revenue flowing into the U.S. Treasury at that point would only be enough to pay the interest on all that debt. Forget the principal. Forget Social Security, Medicare, Medicaid, or anything else in the government's budget. And here's the worst part: in order for us to hit $53 trillion of debt, all Congress has to do is nothing. Is Congress pretty good at doing nothing, Mr. Wheeler?"

Jack laughed bitterly. "I'll say."

"*That* is why David Walker is running around with his hair on fire trying to get the word out. You see, the only way to avoid this fiscal crisis is to either double taxes or cut entitlement programs by half. Which alternative do you think politicians are most likely to try?"

"If history serves as a model, I'd say raising taxes."

"I tend to agree. And that leads us to the fourth and final requirement for our volatility shield account: it has to be tax-free."

"Safe, productive, *and* tax-free?"

"That's right," Jane said. "Imagine the alternative. You spend the next 20 years building a volatility shield in a tax-deferred account. Then, when it comes time to take a distribution, you forfeit 50% to tax. You'd only have enough money to cover six months' worth of living expenses."

"In which case the strategy wouldn't work."

"Exactly."

Jack nodded as the dots began to connect. "So, if it makes sense to grow my volatility shield in a tax-free account, then it almost certainly makes sense to grow all my other retirement savings in tax-free accounts as well, right?"

"That's right. In fact, in a rising tax rate environment, the very best tax bracket is the zero percent tax bracket."

"Why's that?"

"If tax rates double," Jane said with a smile, "two times zero is still zero."

"Makes sense," Jack said, nodding his head. "Okay, let's see if I can summarize: it has to be safe and productive. It needs to be in place before I reach retirement. And it needs to be tax-free."

"Four for four."

"And let me guess. You'll unveil the true identity of the volatility shield tomorrow morning?"

Jane smiled as her eye twinkled. "9 a.m."

CHAPTER 13

Well, if it isn't two of my very favorite people," Jack said as he took his place at the restaurant table.

"Uh, who are you, and what have you done with my brother?" Annie dead-panned.

"Hello, Brian," Jack said, shaking Annie's husband's outstretched hand.

Jack couldn't contain the smile that was smeared across his face.

"You're decidedly more chipper than when I saw you two days ago," Annie said.

"Yeah," Brian said. "All things considered, you're positively glowing."

"As devastating as the news of Ted's health and financial situation have been, there's a small silver lining in all of this."

"Oh?" Annie asked.

"Ted's finances have opened my eyes to the reality that I'm not as prepared for retirement as I thought."

"But you've always been good with your money," Annie objected. "You're not an extravagant spender and, from what you've told me, your retirement plan is on track."

"That's what I thought, too. But after I took another look, I realized that I have a $650,000 shortfall."

"And how did Ted's health crisis crystallize all this for you?" Brian asked.

"The details of Ted's financial picture seemed off, suspiciously so. I didn't feel like I was getting the answers I was looking for from Bruce Lassiter's office, so I sought a second opinion from an advisor across town. She helped me understand why Ted ran out of money and how I can avoid those same mistakes in my own retirement. In fact, what I've been learning over the last few days almost certainly has implications for you guys as well."

"All right," Brian said, genuinely intrigued. "Lay it on us."

"Ted's fatal flaw was a withdrawal rate in retirement that was far too high."

"The combination of market loss and account withdrawals can send your portfolio into a tailspin from which it never recovers," Annie explained, remembering their earlier conversation.

"Good memory," Jack said with a laugh. "That's why financial experts say you should never distribute more than 4% of your starting retirement balance in any given year. For example, if you start with $1,000,000 on the first day of retirement, you should never withdraw more than $40,000 in a year."

"Ah, yes, the 4% rule," Brian said. "You're talking about sequence of return risk."

"Wait, what?" Jack asked. "You've heard of this before?"

Brian shrugged. "I read about it at least once a month in *Kiplinger's* magazine. It's sort of a cardinal rule in retirement planning. Sequence of return risk can kill your portfolio, and the 4% rule is the antidote."

Jack's jaw went slack. He couldn't believe what he was hearing. "You sound like you know a thing or two about retirement planning."

"Not really. I try to read up on these things, but I'm no guru."

"Then you also know that if you're always shackled by the 4% rule, then you have to save a massive amount of money just to fund your lifestyle needs in retirement. For example, if I wanted to live on $100,000 per year in retirement, I'd have to save $2.5 million."

"And the lower your rate of withdrawal, the more you need to save," Brian pointed out.

"Exactly," Jack said, impressed with Brian's firm grasp of the principle. "But what if I told you there was a way to withdraw far more than 4% from your retirement assets and still maintain a high likelihood of never running out of money?"

"I'd want to know more," Brian said. "But I'd also be skeptical."

"From one skeptic to another, I can appreciate that. Let's do this: I'll share the strategy, then you give me your honest assessment."

"Fair enough," Brian said.

Jack cleared his throat before starting. "Every retiree will experience between two and four down years, on average, in the first ten years of their retirement. When you rely on your stock market portfolio during those down years, you dramatically limit your rate of withdrawal. Ergo the 4% Rule."

"Right," Brian confirmed.

"What if you didn't take money out of your stock market portfolio during those years, but instead took money out of a side account that was growing safely and productively? For our purposes, we'll call this account the volatility shield."

"It would give your stock market portfolio a chance to recover," Brian said.

"Precisely. And what if, by so doing, you could liberate yourself from the shackles of the 4% rule and boost your withdrawal rates to 7% or higher?"

Brian's eyes narrowed with skepticism. "So, what kind of investment qualifies as a volatility shield?"

"To qualify, an investment must have a number of important attributes. It has to be safe. You can't very well have a volatility shield that's losing money in the stock market."

"Like a savings account," Annie said.

"A savings account wouldn't do the trick," Jack said. "It violates ground rule two: it must be productive."

"What do you mean by productive?" she asked.

"Four percent to 6% over time," Jack answered.

Now Annie's eyes narrowed skeptically.

Brian shook his head and said, "Sounds a little too good to be true."

"Indulge me," Jack said, pressing forward. "Rule three: your volatility shield must be in place *before* your retirement starts. You can't start funding your volatility shield at retirement, given the possibility that your first few years of distributions could be in a down market."

"Sounds like something you need to start funding years in advance," Brian said.

"That's right," Jack said. "It could take as little as four years to fund the account, but for most people it could take ten years or more. That's part of why ground rule two is so important: the volatility shield must grow productively. If you couldn't grow your volatility shield productively, you'd have to make much larger contributions along the way."

"So," Brian said, "it has to be safe, productive, and firmly in place before retirement starts."

"Excellent summation Brian. That brings us to the final ground rule. The volatility shield must be tax-free. There's good reason to believe that by the time we all retire in 20 years, taxes could be dramatically higher than they are today. If you contribute to your volatility shield at today's low tax rates, you can avoid having to pay taxes at much higher rates down the road."

Brian and Annie were still wearing matching expressions of skepticism.

"What?" Jack asked. "Why aren't you two as excited as I am?"

"The investment you describe doesn't exist," Brian said. "There isn't an investment out there that guarantees against loss while also growing 4% to 6%. Tax-free, no less. Investments have a risk versus reward relationship. For an investment to grow at those rates, you'd *have* to incur some risk. What you describe violates the most fundamental laws of the investment universe."

"That's exactly what *I* said when I first heard about this. But I can promise you this investment *does* exist."

"Then what is it?" Brian pressed.

Heat began to invade Jack's cheeks as he lapsed into silence. After a few awkward seconds, he spoke. "Let me qualify that. I have it on good authority that the investment exists. I find out its identity tomorrow morning. I'll let you know then."

Brian's look of suspicion suddenly melted into a devious smile. "If I didn't know any better, I'd say you just described permanent life insurance."

Jack blinked. "*What?*"

"Yeah. Somebody tried to sell me one of those policies a few years back. Described it exactly how you described this so-called volatility shield. Said that the money inside the policy grew safely and productively, and you could pull it out tax-free. I didn't go for it, of course. I'm more of a term insurance guy myself. Thought you were too, come to think of it. Is this really a road you want to go down?"

Jack felt a burst of defensiveness. If there was one thing the volatility shield was most certainly not, it was permanent life insurance. "There's no way this is—"

"Permanent life insurance?" Brian interrupted. "Fine. Let me ask you a question. Does this advisor of yours *sell* permanent life insurance policies?"

Jack remembered seeing life insurance on Jane's website as well as the brief mention of it during their first conversation. Jane *did* sell life insurance, but it was only in what she'd referred to as "appropriate" situations. Surely, the volatility shield was not a life insurance policy. It couldn't be. Could it?

"I suppose it's possible," Jack muttered. "I find out one way or the other tomorrow," Jack said, hoping to quickly change the subject.

But Brian's accusation soon burrowed deep into Jack's mind. By the time he went to sleep that night, his doubts had metastasized into something much more malignant.

CHAPTER 14

As Jack prepared breakfast in Ted's condo the next morning, he reflected on the exchange he'd had with Jane the first day they'd met. He'd given permanent life insurance a particularly brutal critique, and she'd seemed miffed by it. She'd managed to smile through his lambasting but had quickly moved on to a different subject. Later, after Jane had laid out the five traditional ways to bridge a retirement shortfall, Jack had asked about a sixth way—a less painful strategy—one that would free him from the confines of the 4% rule. But Jane had balked, initially denying that a sixth strategy existed. Later, she'd clarified that such a strategy *did* exist, but made it clear that he was not a good candidate for it. And now he understood why: he'd expressed his distaste for permanent life insurance from the very start.

But Jack had pushed the issue, and she'd agreed to unveil the strategy, but only with the proviso that he discard all of his old "outdated" financial paradigms and maintain an open mind.

And Jack had agreed to do just that. But now it was clear to him that the volatility shield was none other than a permanent life insurance policy. Had he known this was what the strategy called for, he wouldn't have wasted his time. He fumed as he thought about the wasted hours he'd spent in her office, hanging on every word, waiting on pins and needles for the final investment vehicle to be revealed.

Jack's cellphone buzzed in his pocket. He pulled it out and saw that it was a text from Heather at Jane Fletcher's office.

Just confirming your appointment with Jane today at 9 a.m.

He stuffed the phone back in his pocket without responding. He wouldn't be wasting any more of his valuable time with Jane.

Jack continued to brood for another hour before getting down to work. He still had a few things to button up as Ted's financial power of attorney. His first order of business was to determine how close Ted was to qualifying for state Medicaid funding. For the state to pick up the bill, Ted's assets would need to be spent down to $2,000. Currently, there was $71,000 in his stock account, but there was one other account Jack had yet to check: Ted's personal checking account.

Jack pulled a piece of paper out of his briefcase that contained the passwords to a few of Ted's basic accounts: bank, homeowner's insurance, auto insurance, and Social Security. Ted had given Jack this information in the immediate wake of Genevieve's death when he'd agreed to be Ted's financial power of attorney.

Jack pulled up the website for Lancaster Credit Union and entered Ted's login credentials. He navigated to Ted's personal checking account and clicked on it. The balance was $4,562. Ted's savings account had another $200.

After visiting St. Luke's, he'd learned that Ted would be required to pay $7,000 every month until his net worth hit the $2,000 threshold. At that point, the State of North Carolina would begin paying the difference between Ted's Social Security and the total monthly expense, or around $5,000. It was sobering to think that Ted's once vast net worth had been reduced to a grand total of $75,000. And that would be gone in less than a year.

After meeting with Jane, he'd hoped the volatility shield was a foolproof way for him to avoid the same fate, but now he knew better.

Jack was about to power down the computer when something at the bottom of the online bank statement caught his eye. It simply read -$5,000. What was this? Some sort of automatic deduction? Jack scrolled down and discovered that the same deduction had been made every month for the last 12 months.

Who had been subtracting money from Ted's account? Was this one of Ted's splurges? Was this all part of Ted's "letting go" in the wake of Genny's death? Whatever was going on, massive alarm bells were sounding in Jack's head.

Jack scrolled farther to see if he could identify the exact point when the deductions had begun. He scrolled back eight, nine, ten years. The first $5,000 deduction had taken place three months after Genny's death. The timing explained everything. For the last ten years, Ted had been funneling money into a hidden spending account. Ted *had* let go, after all. But why bother keeping it a secret? Whatever the explanation, this much was clear: Ted had blown through $165,000 per year over the last ten years and had next to nothing to show for it. Jack shook his head in disgust.

Jack expanded the window, looking for a number to call. Certainly someone at the bank could explain where all those deductions were going. When the screen expanded, however, it revealed a line of script to the left of the withdrawal he hadn't previously noticed. It said "American Federal…"

What was American Federal? He opened up a Google browser and typed American Federal into the search bar, allowing Google's auto-complete feature to do the rest. Within moments a list of candidates spilled onto his screen:

American Federal *Bank*

American Federal *Credit Union*

American Federal *Mortgage*

American Federal *Holidays*

American Federal *System*

American Federal *Life*

He scanned down the list. Both American Federal Bank and American Federal Credit Union were distinct possibilities. But why would Ted transfer money from one bank to another just so he could spend it? What was he hiding? Something wasn't adding up.

Jack scanned through the other options until he got to the bottom. His eyes lingered on the last name: American Federal Life. Was it a life insurance company? Jack googled it and then pulled up the website. Sure enough, a life insurance company out of Raleigh, North Carolina. He minimized the window, all but dismissing it as a possibility. If there was one thing he and Ted did share, it was their hatred of permanent life insurance.

Jack was at a dead end. Massive amounts of money had been funneled out of Ted's personal checking account over the last ten years, and the only clue he had to go on was American Federal. Jack went back to his original American Federal Google search and checked the list again. This time his eyes hovered over the last option: American Federal Life. He was about to turn off the monitor when, on a whim, he expanded the window for the American Federal Life website. In the upper right-hand corner of the screen, an icon invited him to submit his login credentials.

The username was easy enough. Most companies these days simply asked for an email. Jack shook his head as he typed in *thelegendof lancaster@aol.com*. Even his email address was an attempt to draw attention to an NFL career that had ended over 40 years ago.

The password would prove more difficult. Ted had used the same password for all the accounts on Jack's password sheet, but when he entered it this time, he got a "wrong username/password combination" message. Jack tapped his fingers against the desk as he considered other password combinations. Every attempt produced the same message. He knew the system would lock him out if he kept on guessing at random.

He started rifling through drawers and scanning about the room for evidence of a password. After a few moments, his eyes alighted on the post-it note at the bottom of the computer screen that he'd noticed earlier. It said: "genevieve."

Ted's love for Jack's mother had been fierce. This post-it note was a reminder of that. After staring at it for a moment, however, Jack began to frown. genevieve. genevieve. genevieve. Why had Ted failed to capitalize her name? Jack hadn't noticed the lower-case "g" until now.

Jack plucked the post-it note off the monitor and held it next to the password field on the screen. Could it be this easy? Slowly, he typed in his mother's name, then clicked submit. To Jack's amazement, the site unlocked, revealing a life insurance policy statement.

As he pored over the statement, he could scarcely believe what he was seeing. The total death benefit for the policy appeared to be $1.5 million. Even more surprising was the cash value: $685,000. Jack's heart pounded as he continued to scan the webpage for more details.

After further investigation Ted found another link that said Chronic Illness Rider. This page revealed that Ted's policy had a provision that would allow him to spend up to $1 million of his death benefit in advance of his death for the purpose of paying for long-term care. He only needed to find a doctor who could write a letter stating that Ted could no longer perform two of six activities of daily living. A quick phone call to Dr. Sidwell and that could be arranged.

Jack grew lightheaded as he attempted to process the revelation that had just distilled upon the screen. Was this even possible? Had Ted really been funneling $5,000 per month into a life insurance policy over the last ten years? None of this added up.

Jack collapsed into his chair as he tried to make sense of it all. He felt like he was only observing part of the puzzle. He needed more information. He needed context. He needed to talk with the life insurance agent who sold Ted this policy.

Which he could do. After all, *he* was the financial power of attorney. He had every right to call the life insurance agent to see exactly what had prompted this policy and how Jack could access it to pay for Ted's long-term care. He scanned the navigation bar at the top and clicked on a link that said, "Talk to Your Agent."

He scrolled to the bottom of the screen and nearly fell out of his chair. Ted's life insurance agent was Jane Fletcher.

CHAPTER 15

Jane was sitting at her desk, pushing the remnants of a Caesar salad around her plate when a shadow darkened the doorway to her office. She looked up and saw Jack Wheeler.

"Heather said you might have a moment to chat," Jack said as he stepped into her office.

"I'm busy, Mr. Wheeler. I don't know if I can afford to lose any more time on you. Not after your no-show this morning."

"Just a minute or two. I won't be long."

Jane dropped her fork onto her plate and fixed her mirthless gaze upon Jack. After a few tense moments she gave a slight nod at the chair across from her. "You have five minutes."

Jack slid into the chair, pulled a piece of paper from his pocket and pushed it across the desk. Jane picked it up and began to read.

"How did you get this?" she demanded. "These are the private records of *my* client and it's completely inappropriate that you—"

She stopped when she saw an enigmatic smile spreading across Jack's face.

"Your stepfather…" She shook her head when it finally occurred to her. "Ted Hardy is *your* stepfather?"

Jack's smile widened.

She let out an exasperated chuckle. "Wish I'd known that earlier. It would've saved both of us a whole lot of grief and aggravation."

"Perhaps. But I might not have learned some important and valuable lessons along the way."

She smiled. "You may be right on that count."

Jack's face soon grew serious. "I still feel like there's an aspect of this situation that I'm just not seeing. I was hoping that you could help me piece it together. How did Ted go from an underserved, soon to be bankrupt client of Bruce Lassiter to a financially stable client of Jane Fletcher?"

Jane took a deep breath as her mind transported her back to 2009. It was the day that Ted Hardy had set foot in her office for the *second* time.

*   *   *

Jane had met with clients back-to-back all morning and was looking forward to the same in the afternoon. She had just enough time to dash to the break room, grab her lunch, then eat it at her desk while taking in the latest stock market news. When she returned to her office, she saw a figure sitting there, baseball cap pulled down low. The man turned to face her, lifting up the brim of his hat as he did so. Jane froze in her tracks. It was Ted Hardy.

"*Ted?*"

"Hello, Jane."

"It's…been a long time."

"I haven't set foot in your office in 18 years, Jane. Not since you sold me that term insurance policy."

"I'm so sorry about Genevieve. I've heard so many marvelous things about her."

"Thank you, Jane. I miss her terribly."

Something seemed different about the Ted that now sat in her office. There was nothing brash or vain about him. He seemed subdued and reticent, and had an air of quiet humility about him.

"I'm sorry for dropping by during your lunch hour," he said in hushed tones. "But I really need your help."

"Of course, Ted. How can I be of service?"

He took a deep breath. His eyes seemed to be looking *through* her instead of *at* her. "Last week, I told Bruce Lassiter that I'd begun to look for a new financial advisor. He didn't take it very well…"

Jane hit the intercom on her phone.

"Heather, please hold all my calls."

Her gaze returned to Ted. "Go on," she said.

"We argued. He said he couldn't afford to lose me as a client—made promises that things would improve, told me that he had it all figured out and I just had to be patient. My *average* rates of return would vindicate me in the long run. Jane, my portfolio dropped from $1,600,000 to just under $900,000 in the last year alone. My *average* rates of return are killing me."

Jane nodded her head sympathetically and urged him to continue.

"As I got up to leave, Bruce walked over to the wall, pulled the painting off and revealed a safe. He spun the dial, pulled the safe open and then grabbed a folded piece of paper. It was a letter. Bruce was nice enough to give me a copy."

Ted slid a photocopy of the letter across the desk.

Jane picked it up and began to read:

Dear Mel,

My sources tell me you've begun to refer to me as Scrooge McHardy among members of the community. Now Mel, just because I don't donate money to your worthless cause doesn't make me a Scrooge. Let's make a deal. If you agree to never, ever come into my office looking for freebies and handouts, I'll agree to not sue you for libel and defamation. You don't want to cross me Mel. I will absolutely bury you.

Love, Ted

P.S. Why don't you and the worthless band of misfits you babysit go out and get real jobs? BTW, if you ever step another foot in my office, I will come over here and personally burn this building to the ground.

Jane gasped as the letter fell out of her hands and onto the desk. "You didn't, Ted."

"I did. I'd had too much to drink and I acted impulsively. When I learned what Mel had been saying about me, I just exploded. When I stormed out of my office to confront him, my assistant became concerned. So, she called Bruce and asked him to intervene. When I got to Mel's office, he wasn't there so I wrote that letter and taped it to his door. By the time Bruce got there, I'd already gone. Bruce read the letter and then tucked it into his pocket for safekeeping. Mel never read the letter."

"So, Bruce is using that letter as blackmail?" Jane gasped.

"If I ever left Lassiter Financial, a photocopy of that letter would go straight to Sal Giordano. It would destroy me."

"Oh, Ted. I'm so sorry. What can I do to help?"

"Jane, I'd like *you* to be my financial advisor."

Jane's mouth fell open.

"Uh, Ted, that's impossible. Like you said, Bruce would ruin you."

"I have a plan," Ted insisted. "Any wholesale transfer of assets *will* show up on Bruce's radar. So that's not an option. But I think there may be a backdoor approach."

"A backdoor approach?" Jane said, her eyebrows rising.

"I've been taking $165,000 annual distributions from my account since the very beginning. Bruce has no idea how that money gets spent. With Genny gone, it's just me. I won't be traveling, I can downsize my home, I can live off a fraction of that amount."

"How much are you taking home after tax?"

"About $120,000 per year."

"And how much of that do you need to pay for your lifestyle?"

"Not a lot."

"I need a number, Ted."

"Let's say $60,000 per year."

"So, you need an account in which to invest about $5,000 per month?"

"Yes, and it has to be completely off the radar."

"Confidentiality won't be a problem. What else do you need this account to do for you?"

"I need something that can grow without a lot of risk. I can't afford any more 39% dips."

Jane was scribbling notes on a pad of paper. "Go on."

"I'd *really* like it to be tax-free, but I know that's asking a lot."

"Maybe, maybe not. We'll certainly evaluate all our options."

"I'd also like some sort of long-term care benefit. I spent six months at my wife's bedside. I don't want either of my children to have to do the same for me."

Jane made a note of that on her pad.

"And finally, I want a way to leave a legacy. I've been blinded by my own greed and selfishness for far too long."

"That's asking for a lot, Ted."

"I know, but if there's anyone who can pull this off, it's you. I've been doing my homework, Jane. Word is, you know your stuff, and you're not afraid to get outside the box. More importantly, your character is beyond reproach. I'm just sorry I didn't approach you sooner."

Jane blushed, then took a deep breath.

"To summarize, you want to grow your money safely and productively in a tax-free environment, you want long-term care coverage, *and* you want to pull all this off without Bruce knowing a thing?"

"And to leave a legacy, if it's not too much to ask."

Jane began tapping her pen on her desk as she fell deep into thought. After a few moments, she spoke. "I think I have an idea. But you have to have an open mind."

"I wouldn't be here if I weren't prepared to embrace an outside-the-box strategy."

"Good. Tell me something, Ted, what do you know about permanent life insurance?"

CHAPTER 16

As Jane finished her story, Jack sat slumped in his chair, stunned into silence. Ted hadn't gone on a spending spree over the last ten years. Quite the opposite. He'd dramatically reduced his lifestyle as part of a secret asset-shifting arrangement with Jane. That explained everything: the missed appointments with Bruce, the unopened statements, and the lapsed term life insurance policy. It also explained Ted's insistence on withdrawing $165,000 from his portfolio every year like clockwork. Even more startling, Ted had undergone some sort of metamorphosis in the wake of Genevieve's death. Is that what Annie had been trying to communicate all these years?

"You're telling me," Jack finally managed to say, "that you were able to meet every one of Ted's needs through the implementation of a permanent life insurance policy?"

"You already know the answer to that question, Mr. Wheeler. Ted needed safe and productive growth in a tax-free environment. Check, check, and check. He also wanted a long-term care rider and a death benefit for legacy. Double check. Do you know of any other vehicle that could have accomplished all five of those things?"

Permanent life insurance. Jack had been so leery of it over the years that he almost couldn't bring himself to admit that it had been the lynchpin in Jane's ingenious plan. Jack thought back to all the books and websites he'd read. Nothing even came close.

"I will tentatively admit that permanent life insurance was the right fit for Ted in *this* instance," Jack said. "But I'm not so sure that permanent life insurance is right for me. And I'm pretty sure that's where you were headed with this whole volatility shield discussion."

"And that's why you stood me up this morning?" Jane asked.

Jack nodded sheepishly.

"I *was* surprised when you didn't show up. Given your concerns over the 4% rule, I'd thought you'd at least be interested in seeing the solution."

"I'm only interested in solutions that are vindicated by math. I'm not interested in solutions that only sound good in theory. I'm an engineer, Jane. The math *has* to add up."

"Why would I make a recommendation to you that wasn't corroborated by math? Take a look at that wall." Jane pointed off to her right. A diploma from UNC Chapel Hill hung on the wall.

Jack looked closely at the diploma. "You did your undergraduate in mathematics?"

She nodded. "We're kindred spirits, Mr. Wheeler. I require the same empirical proof that you do. *All* my recommendations are driven by data."

"Are you saying that there's mathematical proof that a permanent life insurance policy can help free me from the 4% rule?"

Jane pulled a folder out of the lateral file behind her and opened it on her desk. "When you're bound by the 4% rule, you fall short of your retirement goals by roughly $650,000. If you do it your way, you'll have to save more, spend less, work longer, die sooner, or take more risk in the market."

"Thanks for the reminder."

"*However*, if we incorporate a volatility shield—"

"You mean permanent life insurance," Jack interrupted.

"If we incorporate permanent life insurance," Jane continued without missing a beat, "your outlook changes dramatically. Are you sure you want to see these numbers, Jack?"

"Only if they add up."

"Here's the recommendation I was prepared to give you this morning. Reduce your current $19,000 contribution to your 401(k) down to the 3% match. That means both you and your employer will be contributing $4,500 per year which frees up the other $14,500."

"But that's a pre-tax number, right?"

"Yes, so we pay tax at a combined state and federal rate of 30%, and that leaves us with $10,150 per year."

Jack had a scowl on his face, but he nodded for her to go on.

"We would then contribute that $10,150 every year for the next 20 years to a permanent life insurance policy on you. That would put over $375,000 in your volatility shield by the time you retire. That's enough to fund five full years of after-tax living expenses."

"What does that do to my rate of withdrawal?"

"According to our Monte Carlo Simulations, you could take 8% withdrawals with 95% confidence your money would last until life expectancy."

Jack's scowl only deepened. "If I take money that was destined for my 401(k) and contribute it to a permanent life insurance policy instead, I *might* have five years' worth of living expenses accumulated. But I would also have much less in my 401(k). So, even if I could withdraw 8% from my 401(k), it would be on a much smaller balance."

"You're right. Your 401(k) balance at retirement would be $1,258,986. What's 8% of $1,258,986, Mr. Wheeler?"

Jack grumbled as he pulled out his phone to do the calculation. When he saw the number, the scowl on his face melted away.

"I can't believe it. $100,718," Jack said, visibly shocked.

"Furthermore, your contributions to your volatility shield will now begin to grow safely and productively."

"Four percent to 6% over time," Jack said.

"Indeed. And, for that reason, your volatility shield could serve as the bond portion of your overall portfolio. To compensate, you'd want to increase the stock allocation in your 401(k)."

"If I took more risk in my 401(k), I could potentially have even more than $1,258,986 at retirement."

"In which case, you just gave yourself a raise."

Jack relaxed in his chair as relief washed over him. He now had a 95% chance of his money lasting until life expectancy without resorting to any of the five painful approaches they had discussed earlier.

"Here's the moral of the story Mr. Wheeler. You don't have to love permanent life insurance. You just have to like it a little bit more than you like the 4% rule. Because in the end, the only way to vanquish the 4% rule and hit your retirement goals is to fully fund a volatility shield by the time you reach 65."

"I…I don't know what to say. I've never been so happy to be so wrong."

"Congratulations, Mr. Wheeler. You just freed yourself from the 4% rule."

Jane reached across the table to offer him a congratulatory handshake. But Jack just stared at the offered hand, letting it hang there in the air. Her cheerful smile began to fade as her hand fell limply to the desk. Jack studied her for one last moment, then rose from his chair, marched around the table and enveloped her in an enormous hug.

"Thank you for everything you've done for me and my family, Jane Fletcher," Jack whispered in her ear. "We owe you an enormous debt of gratitude."

"I haven't done anything for you yet, Mr. Wheeler. You still have to qualify."

Surprised, Jack pulled out of the hug. "Qualify? What do I have to do?"

Jane looked at her watch and grimaced. "I'm afraid we're out of time for today. But if you can be here tomorrow morning at 9, we'll get the health examination process started."

Jack frowned at the thought of having to wait another 24 hours before beginning the process of securing his retirement. But he'd waited this long. What was another day?

"Not a problem," Jack said, turning toward the door of her office. But, as he crossed the threshold of her office, his brow furrowed. There was one detail of Ted's plan that he hadn't yet considered. He turned back to Jane. "Who did Ted name as the beneficiary?"

Jane smiled. "I thought you'd never ask."

CHAPTER 17

Two days later, Jack was finally ready to go home. The day before, he'd begun the underwriting process with Jane and then submitted the proper documentation to access the death benefit via the Chronic Illness Rider on Ted's policy. It had been a roller coaster ride of a week, but its finale had exceeded all of his wildest expectations.

Jack grabbed his suitcases, pulled up the zipper on his jacket, and strode toward the front door of Ted's tiny condominium. When he pulled the door open, that morning's edition of the *Lancaster Gazette* lay at his feet. He picked it up and threw it onto the counter but, as he did so, the paper flopped open revealing the headline just below the fold. It read: *Local Football Legend Ted Hardy Dead Broke.* The subtitle read: *After Aneurism, Ted Hardy to Spend Remaining Years at St. Luke's.* The article was written by Sal Giordano.

Anger flickered within Jack as he grabbed his phone and found the number for the *Lancaster Gazette*. He pressed dial.

"Lancaster Gazette," came the voice on the other end.

"Sal Giordano," Jack said through clenched teeth.

"One moment please."

The phone went silent for a moment.

"Sal Giordano."

"Sal, it's Jack Wheeler."

"Jack Wheeler," he said with a chuckle. "To what do I owe the pleasure?"

"Your article about my stepfather is wrong. Disastrously so. The retraction and ensuing lawsuit will be painful. You'll be lucky if any paper will hire you by the time Ted's attorneys are done."

Sal laughed contemptuously.

"I gave you the chance to spin the article whatever way you wanted. This is what happens when you ignore me, Jack. *I* get to shape the narrative. And no, there won't be any retractions. That article is rock solid. Ted Hardy is as broke now as he was the day he came into the world."

"My stepfather is not broke," Jack spat. "And if you don't submit a retraction immediately, this will be the last article you ever write."

"Oh, Jack. Let's dispense with the threats. I have ample proof that Ted Hardy *is* dead broke. What's more, I photographed you walking out of the only Medicaid-funded long-term care facility in town. Did you see the photo? You really do look quite dashing."

Jack tore open the paper and saw a black and white photo of him walking out of St. Luke's four days earlier. The caption read, "Jack Wheeler exits St. Luke's where his stepfather Ted Hardy will soon become a tenant."

Jack let out a long, slow breath. "I'll admit it: in my haste to get Ted settled, I overlooked a few details of his finances. It really was careless of me. But after further investigation, I found that my stepfather managed to accumulate quite the substantial nest egg after all. And when you have that kind of money, you have options. The first option Ted's attorneys will be exercising, of course, is to sue you and your paper into oblivion."

There was silence on the other end of the phone.

"But I saw you," Sal stammered. "I *saw* you walking out of St. Luke's."

"Expect a warmly worded letter from Ted's attorney by the end of the week. Goodbye, Sal."

"Wait!" Sal said, his voice laced with desperation. "I'll write a retraction just like you wanted. It'll be out by tomorrow morning."

"That's a good start, Sal. But there's one other thing I'd like you to do for me."

"Anything."

"There's a breaking story out of Bruce Lassiter's office. I'm going to need you to investigate it."

EPILOGUE

One month later

Mr. Wheeler,

I appreciate the scoop on Bruce Lassiter. I'm glad to see there aren't any hard feelings between us. I attached the article. I thought you should be the first to read it.

Sal Giordano

Jack clicked on the attachment.

Local Money Manager Submits to Authorities

By Sal Giordano

Local money manager Bruce Lassiter turned himself into authorities yesterday after a private investigation revealed he had threatened to blackmail former NFL quarterback, and Lancaster resident, Ted Hardy. Sources have confirmed that Lassiter threatened blackmail when Hardy broached the subject of moving his assets to another advisor following the market downturn in 2008. The investigation revealed that Hardy's celebrity had been a driving force behind the growth of Lassiter's practice since the year 2000, and Lassiter feared Hardy's departure would lead to a mass reduction in his clientele.

According to sources, Lassiter also encouraged his clients to take

unsustainable withdrawals regardless of market conditions. Lassiter
likewise placed undue emphasis on his average annual rates of
return. This story is developing.

Two Years Later

Two years after entering Sunset Senior Care, Ted Hardy died. Jack took
three days off work to fly back for the funeral. But Ted's funeral wasn't
Jack's only motivation for returning to Lancaster. As Ted's financial
power of attorney, and executor of his estate, he wanted to oversee
the last, defining gesture of Ted's life. It was a plan that had been in
motion for nearly 12 years.

Four suit-clad men got out of a car and strode into a rundown
building in downtown Lancaster. The smell of potatoes and stale bread
hung heavy in the air. Off in one corner, dirty pots were stacked in a
sink. Another corner had pallets of carrots, potatoes, and other veg-
etables. The men saw a square of light cast against the back wall and
walked toward it.

They came to a door that had a sign to the left of it which read
Mel Kauffman, Director.

Jack knocked lightly on the glass.

After a moment, the door swung open and an older and greyer
version of Mel Kauffman stood before them. He gave the four men in
front of him a nervous smile. "Gentlemen, if you're from the bank, I
can explain. It's just that—"

"Mel, it's me. Jack Wheeler, remember?"

Recognition swept across Mel's face soon followed by relief and a
warm embrace.

"Jack, what on earth brings you to these parts? I haven't seen you
in years!"

Jack smiled, then turned to make the introductions. "Mel, I'd
like to introduce Max Arnett. He's an attorney here in town. Mike
Caldwell is an architect, one of the best in the business. Stan Markowitz
is a representative of a company called American Federal Life out of
Raleigh, North Carolina."

"Nice to meet you all," Mel said, still visibly shaken. "I'm afraid our soup line closed over two hours ago. Otherwise, I'd offer you something to eat."

"We're not here for food, Mel. We're here to talk about Ted Hardy."

Mel's nervous grin fell into a frown.

"Ted died about ten days ago," Jack continued.

"Condolences," Mel said, his insincerity palpable.

"There was a particular provision in his estate plan that I'd like to bring to your attention," Jack said. "About 12 years ago, Ted took out a life insurance policy. Max, you want to take it from here?"

"The beneficiary of the life insurance policy was the 'Ted Hardy Revocable Living Trust,'" Max said. "And the sole beneficiary of the Ted Hardy Revocable Living Trust is the Lancaster Boys Club."

"That's great," Mel said dully, before lapsing into silence.

After a moment of awkward silence, Mel continued. "I'm sorry, Jack. I'm grateful, but I'm afraid it's too late. The building on Newton has already been condemned. They tear it down next month. A little bit of money isn't going to save it now."

"Keep listening Mel," Jack urged.

"Now, I have to warn you," Max told Mel, "some of Ted's death benefit was spent over the last two years to pay for his long-term care expenses, but the Lancaster Boys Club is legally entitled to the remaining amount. The final death benefit comes to over $1.4 million."

Mel continued to stare blankly at the man for a few moments before his eyes slowly widened. "How is this possible? This—this can't be right."

"As a representative of American Federal Life," Stan Markowitz chimed in, "I can assure you that figure is correct."

Mel's lower lip began to quiver. Before long, tears were peeling down his cheeks, his shoulders heaving up and down. He dabbed at his tears with a tissue before enveloping each of the men in a deep embrace. Soon, the rest of them were drawing handkerchiefs from their pockets and wiping at their eyes.

After the hugs abated, Jack spoke. "There are provisions in the trust that stipulate exactly how this money is to be spent." With that, the architect Mike Caldwell pulled a rolled-up sheet out of a portable tube he'd been carrying at his side and unfurled it onto the desk in Mel's office.

"Per the language of the trust, I created a plan that fully modernizes the facility," Mike said. "I'm certain you're going to like it."

As Mel took in the renovation plans for the youth facility, the tears returned. Mel had spent the last 40 years of his life dedicated to the troubled youth of Lancaster, battling financial struggle after financial struggle. But this final chapter would be a glorious one.

After marveling over the plans for several moments, Mel finally spoke. "I love the new plans. I mean, I *really* love them. But there's one detail I would change."

He grabbed a pen off his desk and put a big "X" through "Lancaster Boys Club" at the top of the plans. Below it he wrote, "The Ted Hardy Community Center."

"There," Mel said with a smile. "Now it's perfect."

The End

ACKNOWLEDGMENTS

I am thankful for my two chief editors William Crowl and Sara Butler whose sharp eyes and knack for storytelling helped round this story out and polish off its rough edges. I am likewise grateful to the legions of financial advisors from across the country who served as beta readers and gave valuable insight and feedback through this story's many iterations. Their contributions have been indispensable.

I am above all thankful to my wife who has stood by my side for nearly twenty years, laboring long hours, often in my absence, engaged in the vitally important work of raising our seven children. I am grateful that she chose me.

For bulk discounts, go to
thepowerofzerobook.com

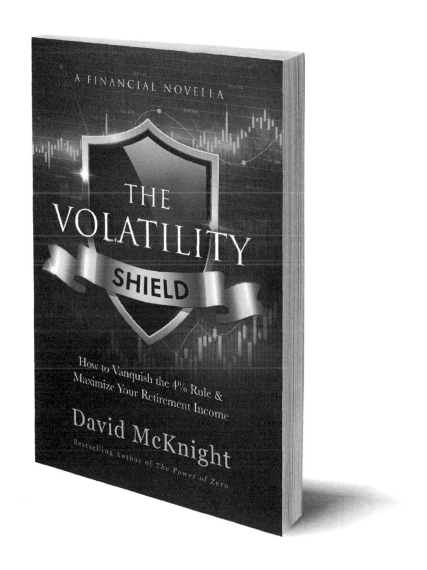

For bulk discounts, go to
thevolatilityshield.com

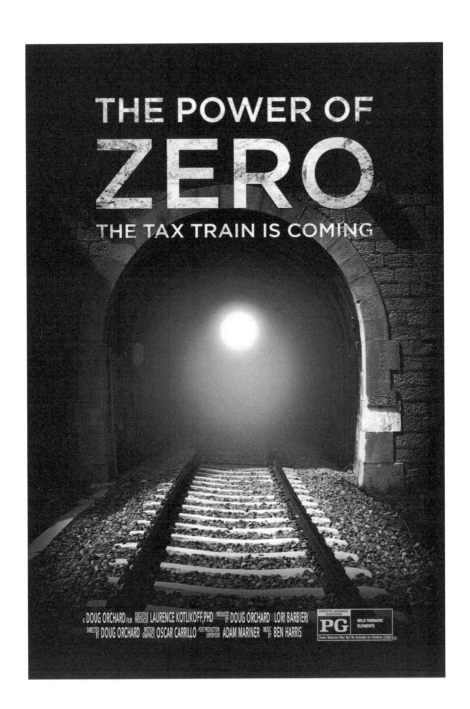

Available on DVD, Blu-ray, and Digital HD on April 23rd, 2019

ABOUT THE AUTHOR

 David McKnight graduated from Brigham Young University with Honors in 1997. Over the past 20 years David has helped put thousands of Americans on the road to the zero percent tax bracket. He has made frequent appearances in *Forbes, USA Today, New York Times, Fox Business, CBS Radio, Bloomberg Radio, Huffington Post, Reuters, CNBC, Yahoo Finance, Nasdaq.com, Investor's Business Daily, MarketWatch* and numerous other national publications. His bestselling book *The Power of Zero* has sold over 185,000 copies and the updated and revised version was published by Penguin Random House. When it was launched in September of 2018, it finished the week as the #2 most-sold business book in the world. This book was recently made into a full-length documentary film, also entitled *The Power of Zero*. As the President of David McKnight & Company, he mentors hundreds of financial advisors from across the country who specialize in the Power of Zero retirement approach. He and his wife Felice have seven children.